Idaho

Echoes in Time

Traveling Idaho's History and Geology

Stories, Directions, Maps, and More

by
R. G. Robertson

Photos by
Karen A. Robertson

tamarack books inc.

First Edition: April 1998
10 9 8 7 6 5 4 3 2 1

ISBN 1-886609-12-8

Maps by Kelly Perry

Published by:

tamarack books inc.

PO Box 190313
Boise, ID 83719-0313
1-800-962-6657

Printed in the United States of America

DEDICATION

Dedicated to the People of Idaho—
Past and Present

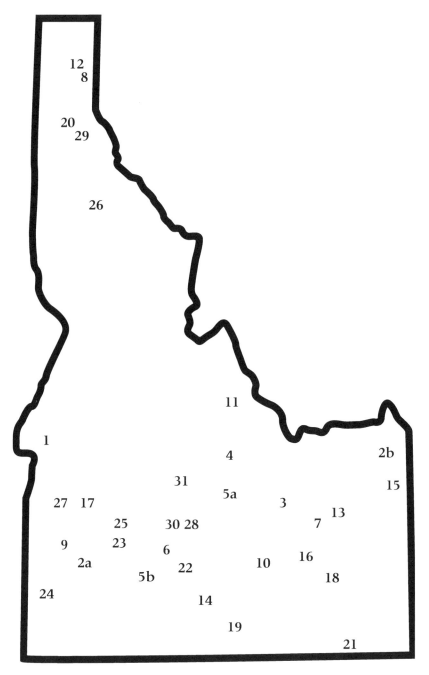

Numbers correspond to chapters.

TABLE OF CONTENTS

ACKNOWLEDGMENTS

I wish to thank the staff at the Community Library in Ketchum, Idaho, and especially Cecilia Cavanaugh in the Regional History Department. I also thank the volunteers at the Idaho Historical Library in Boise.

INTRODUCTION

I'm a trivia junkie. Unusual facts, bizarre statistics, minutiae, the really weird stuff—I find it all fascinating. Consequently for me, Idaho is heaven.

When my wife, Karen, and I moved to Idaho, I knew little about the state beyond Sun Valley's ski runs. But as I began to read about Idaho and explore Idaho's historical sites and unique natural landmarks—places like the City of Rocks, Craters of the Moon, Thousand Springs, Lemhi Pass, Borah Peak, the Teton Basin—I quickly realized that the Gem State was a trivia-lover's paradise.

When I learned that there was enough water in the Snake River Plain Aquifer to cover the entire state to a depth of four feet and that 20,000 years ago a wall of water over 2,000 feet high scoured Idaho's panhandle, my mind went wild with comparisons. For example, empty the aquifer into the Mediterranean Sea, and it'll rise three and one-half inches. And 2,000 feet of water—that's as though someone stacked up two Chrysler Buildings—you remember, the New York skyscraper that King Kong climbed while clutching Fay Wray in the 1933 movie. The possibilities for illustration are endless.

As did most of my generation, I grew up on television and comic-book tales of Wyatt Earp and Bat Masterson. When I first came across the unlikely name "Orlando 'Rube' Robbins," little did I suspect that it belonged to an Idaho lawman whose exploits as a pistoleer equaled in every way those of his more famous contemporaries.

Another of my tidbits resulted from a trip to Boise during the springtime. After driving past acres of blue camas west of Fairfield, I sought to find out more about this lovely flower that each May and June carpets so many of the state's marshes. During my research, I was surprised to discover that this innocent lily had ignited a bloody Indian war.

As I related the things I was learning about Idaho to my long-suffering friends—including some who had lived here all their lives—I saw a void. Many who would normally roll their eyes at the mention of history or geology said "I didn't know that," as they listened to how the Astorians abandoned their canoes at the falls of Caldron Linn. Afterwards, a few of my friends pressed me for directions so they could visit the Snake River's most southern point, where the volcanic walls squeeze the boiling current into a forty-foot-wide gap.

Thinking that other Idahoans might have an interest in the state's past, I began writing a newspaper column called "Idaho Inside Out." Since mid-1995, my stories have appeared regularly in the Idaho Falls *Post Register* and Pocatello *Idaho State Journal,* and a few have been carried in the Burley *South Idaho Press* and Coeur d'Alene *Idaho Spokesman-Review.*

Karen Robertson, who is a freelance photographer, and I always visit the subject locales so she can shoot pictures showing how the sites appear now. Our journeys have taken us from Porthill to Franklin and from Weiser to

Driggs. Yet the more we travel, the more I realize how much there is that still begs to be told.

From my first article through my most recent, my goal has been to make the past come alive. I want my stories to awaken an interest in the reader, to prompt him or her to hike up the Menan Buttes or stroll along a remnant of the Mullan Road. I don't intend *Idaho Echoes in Time* to be an encompassing history or geology textbook. Instead, it's a series of stories about the myriad people and geologic events that collectively contribute to what we call Idaho.

Idaho Echoes in Time is divided in two sections. Part 1: A Land Formed by Fire and Flood is a series of essays or, as I like to think of them, snapshots that trace the corporeal formation of Idaho. If read in sequence, these chapters will recount the state's geologic life, from its separation from the supercontinent Pangaea 250 million years ago, to its adolescence as it grew in area and height, its middle age when it was sculpted by lava, and its mature years when rivers of water and ice carved deep canyons in its earthly flesh.

"Idaho's Swath of Fire" is perhaps the most controversial chapter in this section. While most geologists agree that the Snake River Plain was formed when the North American Plate slid over a permanent "hot spot" in the earth's mantle, not all of them think the hot spot was created seventeen million years ago by a large meteorite that blasted an enormous hole in southeastern Oregon. Whether or not this theory will eventually be proven remains to be seen.

The scope of *Idaho Echoes in Time* has dictated that I omit certain pieces in Idaho's geologic puzzle. But in my defense, let me repeat that it was never my intention to write a classical text. Rather, I want my stories to paint a mosaic that will awaken an interest to further study in the non-geologist reader.

Part 2: A People Forged by Courage looks at Idaho's transients and kinsmen through snippets of time, beginning with Lewis and Clark and continuing until Jim Curran and the construction of the Sun Valley Resort. Rather than write about the pillars of government or industry, I've chosen among the state's many visitors, immigrants and Native Americans, seeking those who have done something memorable, whether good or bad. A few, like Ira Perrine, have left a lasting mark, while others, such as Al Faussett, have had no more influence than a wisp of smoke. Yet no matter how big or small their roles, without their contributions, Idaho would not be what it is today.

The stories in Part 2 are presented chronologically, but unlike those in Part 1, it's unnecessary to read them in sequence in order to grasp some larger understanding of Idaho's history. As the bibliography demonstrates, I've gathered my material from numerous sources, many of which offer differing reports of the same events. For example, in researching Peg Leg Annie, I read a clipping that said she had only one foot amputated and another that said two. I've also read at least two versions about where her rescuers found her after the blizzard that frostbit her feet ended. In deciding what is correct in this tale and in others, I've employed corroborating articles, logic, and occasionally, an educated guess. I ask the reader to consider this when one of my stories disagrees with an account he or she has seen elsewhere.

In a similar vein, historical events may be given different interpretations. For the most part, the opening of the American west has been written from the perspective of white civilization rather than from that of the Native Americans. Revisionist historians have sought to redress this imbalance by blaming Anglo-society for every ill that has befallen the Indians since the days of Christopher

Columbus. Certainly the "dead white males" who settled (or stole, depending on one's view) Idaho, did much to harm Indian culture, but the modern reader would do well to examine past actions in light of the mores of the times.

Idaho Echoes in Time will not settle this dispute. That isn't its goal. It seeks neither to be an apologist for white transgression nor to ignore the plight of the native tribes that were crushed by the influx of soldiers, miners, farmers, and shopkeepers. I've attempted to write my stories objectively, giving the views and motivations of all parties on an issue, then letting the reader determine right from wrong. I trust I've succeeded.

Finally, I've included an addendum to each of the chapters, providing directions to the pertinent sites so the reader can visit them. I've also described activities and scenic points that will make the visits meaningful as well as fun. I urge everyone to see as much of Idaho as he or she can. Gazing on the Snake River Plain from atop Big Southern Butte and peering down at Hells Canyon from Sheep Rock in the Seven Devils Mountains are experiences that I'll always cherish. If this book gets just one person to stand on the cliff above Caldron Linn or to pull off the highway and read a state historical sign, it will have accomplished its purpose.

PART ONE

A Land
Formed by
Fire and Flood

1

McCall:
Idaho's Surf City

Imagine driving to the western limits of McCall and looking not at green forests but at crashing, saltwater waves and endless miles of Pacific beach. Geologists tell us such a scene is exactly what we would have seen had we been alive 250 million years ago.

At that time central Idaho formed the western edge of Pangaea, a supercontinent that included most of North and South America, Europe, Africa and Asia. Beyond Idaho's shoreline stood a vast ocean, dotted with islands and the remnants of other continents that had long since broken apart. Eastward was nothing but land, all the way to China and Siberia.

Then a rift formed in the earth's mantle, and the North and South American plates began drifting west, much like two logs breaking free from a large raft. As the pieces floated apart on a belt of molten rock deep within the earth, the Atlantic Ocean spread—at one or two inches per year—filling the gulf with water.

At the mid-Atlantic Ridge where the split occurred, lava oozed from the earth's mantle, forming new oceanic crust as the sea floor widened. Simultaneously, over near

McCall and all along Idaho's western border, the Pacific crust began sinking into a trench beneath the advancing but more buoyant North American plate.

As the Pacific Ocean grew smaller, the islands and continental debris that littered its surface slid toward Idaho. Being too light to sink, they slammed against the west coast and stuck. The Seven Devils Mountains of the Hells Canyon Wilderness are volcanic Pacific islands that welded to Idaho 100 million years ago. With each succeeding collision, Idaho has inched farther and farther inland.

Meanwhile, these collisions and the subduction of the Pacific crust acted much like two throw rugs bumping together on a slick hardwood floor. The North American plate began to fracture, wrinkle and fold, forming the Rocky Mountains.

As the Pacific crust submerged, it melted the North American plate's basement rocks, forcing granite magma up into the wrinkled welts. As a result, Idaho began pushing skyward.

Then just when the state was becoming a mountaineer's dream, these unstable chunks—some in the Frank Church-River of No Return Wilderness nearly a dozen miles thick—slipped east into Montana. As they moved, they bunched the land before them into even more mountains. Having lost all that weight, Idaho popped up like an empty river barge. However, her new peaks were only half as tall as the ones she had shed.

Today, the North American plate continues to drift toward Hawaii. In time, Oahu and Maui will fuse with California, Oregon and Washington, and Idahoan surfers will have even farther to drive before they can catch a wave.

* * * * *

**Hells Canyon and the Snake River from the
Seven Devils Mountains.**

SEVEN DEVILS MOUNTAINS: From US 95 in Council, take the Hornet Creek Road (later called the Council-Cuprum Road) 29 miles west to Bear Junction, turning left toward Cuprum. In 7.2 miles swing right at the T and drive 1 mile to Cuprum. Continue on another 10.4 miles to the Kinney Point turnoff. The single-lane track to the point (0.5 miles) is rough but possible for cars. Sheep Rock, a National Natural Landmark, is 2.2 miles beyond Kinney Point Road. Hells Canyon and the Seven Devils can be seen from both locations.

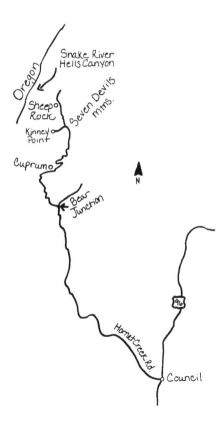

2

IDAHO'S SWATH OF FIRE

Stretching across southern Idaho like the upper torso of a medieval dragon, the Snake River Plain reaches its fiery snout into Yellowstone National Park. Even a cursory glance at the state's topography illustrates that this sweep of land is unique.

If not for the Snake River Plain, Idaho's mountains would extend uninterrupted from Porthill into Nevada and Utah. Yet in a broad swath from the Owyhee River past Jerome and Rexburg and on toward the Continental Divide, the country lies flat, as though bladed by a giant bulldozer.

Some geologists theorize that a massive meteorite struck southeastern Oregon about seventeen million years ago. The force of its impact rent the earth's crust, punching a hole in the mantle. That hole or "hot spot" released an avalanche of basalt magma, which flooded into eastern Washington and the lowlands of western Idaho, creating the Columbia Plateau.

Near the same time, enormous faults began splitting the Rocky Mountains of western Idaho and north-central Nevada. As these rifts pulled apart the earth's crust, long, generally north-south running sections of bedrock started to rise and fall, forming the valleys and mountains called "Basin and Range."

Meanwhile, the North American plate continued drifting west, as it had been doing for well over 200 million years. Being in the mantle, the hot spot didn't move. Instead, much like an acetylene torch held stationary beneath a sliding sheet of steel, the hot spot seared a path across southern Idaho at one and one-half inches per year. Today, it smolders under Yellowstone National Park.

Scientists have traced the hot spot by the enormous resurgent calderas—collapsed volcanoes—it has left in its wake. From Grasmere to Magic Reservoir to Mud Lake to upper Henry's Fork, their ages grow progressively younger.

In Fremont County, the Island Park Caldera measures nearly twenty miles across. Ash from its first outburst 2.1 million years ago blanketed the countryside with enough rhyolite to produce 600 Mount St. Helens eruptions. So hot was the discharge, it congealed into a thick layer of pinkish-gray stone. Such energy and the devastation it wrought are unknown in the modern world, even in the nuclear age.

Under Yellowstone National Park, the hot spot has so far ignited three explosions, the most recent 600,000 years ago. Few geologists think that will be the last. With a 600,000-year interval separating each of the three eruptions, another is certainly due.

Just as the hot spot has seemed to move east, so has the Basin and Range faulting. The shield volcanoes that coated the Snake River Plain with its basalt veneer are a recent consequence of this faulting. Presently, the leading edge of the Basin and Range has entered Utah's Wasatch Mountains, a point directly south of the Yellowstone Caldera.

As for the future of the Snake River Plain, it will continue to grow. So long as the North American plate drifts across the Pacific, the hot spot will kindle its way to central Montana.

* * * * *

BRUNEAU CANYON OVERLOOK: From Mountain Home, follow State Highway 51 south 20 miles to Bruneau; turn left on Hot Springs Road. In 7.8 miles where the pavement ends, keep left on Clover Creek Road; in another 8.1 miles, turn right at the sign for the Bruneau Canyon Overlook, 3.2 miles beyond.

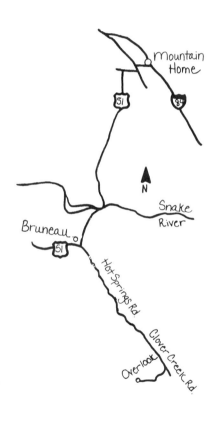

Thought to have been named for Baptiste Bruneau, who trapped here in the early 1800s, the Bruneau River has cut an 800-foot gorge through the basalt and rhyolite of the Bruneau-Jarbridge Caldera. Hikes along the canyon rim, up- and downstream from the overlook, offer stunning views of the river as well as the high desert. During the late spring and early summer, watch for kayakers running the Bruneau's white water. Also, beware of rattlesnakes.

ISLAND PARK CALDERA: About 10 miles north of Ashton, US 20 climbs Big Bend Ridge, a U-shaped rim of rhyolite that partially encircles the Island Park Caldera. Totaling approximately 350 square miles, this dead volcano is the world's largest "recognized" caldera. The highway cuts the crater's northern boundary near Island Park.

While driving across the caldera, observe its western escarpment, which rises 1,200 feet above the Snake River Plain. The caldera's eastern lip lies beneath more recent lava flows from Yellowstone National Park. During the Island Park Caldera's initial eruption 2.1 million years ago, it rained hot ash over an area the size of New Jersey. Following the volcano's smaller, final explosion 800,000 years later, its magma chamber collapsed, forming the enormous basin that is visible today.

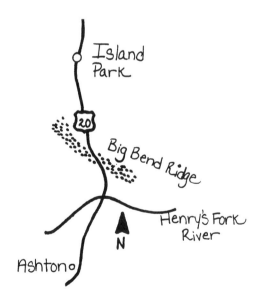

3

You Can See Forever

Viewed from atop Big Southern Butte near Arco, the upper Snake River Plain appears to heave and roll like some sort of primeval, petrified ocean. On a clear day you can see the Teton Mountains painting a steel-gray backdrop for the eastern horizon. To the north the White Knobs, Lost Rivers, Lemhis and Beaverheads resemble giant ribs arching out from Idaho's flat, lava-rippled belly.

If you look west from Idaho Falls, Big Southern and its lessor neighbors, Middle and East buttes, interrupt the landscape much the way volcanic islands break the monotony of the sea. As you gaze over the plain, these mounds of rhyolite seize your eye as though they were magnets.

During the early nineteenth century, the buttes guided fur trappers such as Jedediah Smith and Alexander Ross. A few years later, Oregon-bound emigrants stared at them for hour after endless hour as their exhausted oxen trudged over hoof-splitting rocks.

Today, US 26 parallels Goodale's Cutoff of the Oregon Trail as it knifes between Big Southern and the smaller twins. From inside an air-conditioned car speeding past Atomic City, Middle and East buttes appear impressive.

But from the 7,560-foot summit of Big Southern, they look as imposing as dwarf pine alongside a Sequoia redwood.

Although geologically modern, the buttes trace their ancestry back five or six million years, when violent rhyolitic volcanism erupted across the eastern Snake River Plain. As the North American plate drifted westward, the hotspot that produced these eruptions gradually moved under Yellowstone. Taking their place was a milder form of volcanism that began when the earth's upper mantle started to melt thirty-one to thirty-seven miles below the surface. Like spilled molasses on a warm day, basalt magma oozed from cracks in the plain until it spread a black crust over the rhyolite.

Then, 600,000 years ago in an anticlimactic conclusion to the caldera era of the Snake River Plain, a dome of rhyolite, much like an expanding pressure ridge on an

Spring snow on Big Southern Butte.

asphalt highway, elbowed its way through the basalt and formed East Butte. Middle Butte followed, but with less force. Its rhyolitic summit lies buried under a mountain of basalt.

In a final hurrah around 300,000 years ago, Big Southern Butte thrust its bulk into the daylight. It climbed slowly without the explosive fanfare of early rhyolitic eruptions, almost as though it were an exhausted giant struggling to shrug its massive shoulders. When the forces driving it stopped, Big Southern Butte loomed 2,500 feet above the surrounding plain. Rivers of molten basalt have continued to flood across Big Southern's domain, some even lapping at its base. The last one welled out of Idaho's Great Rift about the time Julius Caesar was born.

Now a National Natural Landmark, Big Southern Butte provides unimpeded views for nearly 100 miles. Whether you drive the jeep road to the top or hike up one of the butte's crumbly flanks, the panorama is worth the effort.

*　*　*　*　*

BIG SOUTHERN BUTTE: From I-15 Exit 93 near Blackfoot, drive northwest 29 miles on US 26, turning west at the sign for Atomic City; for those coming from Arco, the turnoff is 6.8 miles southeast of the US 20/26 junction. Follow the paved spur road 1.4 miles to a T at the edge of town. Turn left (south) for 1.3 miles, then right on a gravel road. After 3.9 miles, cross the Union Pacific railroad tracks. From here on, the road varies between dirt and cinder. In 1 mile bear left and drive another 8.7 miles around the Butt's south and west sides. At the signed intersection, swing right toward Big Butte Lookout. In 3.6 miles come to a ranch and Frenchman's Cabin. Turn right up the Big Butte Lookout jeep road. It is 4.6 extremely rough miles to the summit. Should you choose to hike up one of the Butte's flanks, be aware the rock is loose.

The road to the top of Big Southern Butte is recommended for high clearance, 4-wheel-drive vehicles only. All of Idaho's desert roads can be treacherous when wet. Always carry a backcountry map and emergency supplies, including water.

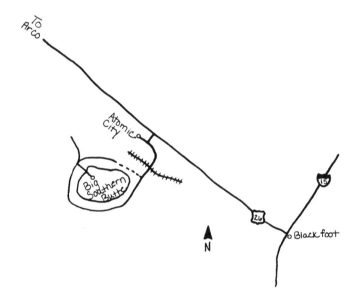

4

GROWING A MOUNTAIN

At 8:06 Friday morning, October 28, 1983, Hilda Goddard was slicing vegetables in her kitchen a few miles from the Mackay Reservoir when she heard a noise that sounded like a low-flying jet fighter. At the same time a dozen miles farther north, Wiley Smith was enjoying a last sip of coffee before heading out to work. In the next instant, their world began to shake.

In the Goddard home, cans and jars jumped off their shelves. Hilda's elderly mother lay in bed, too disoriented to stand. Outside, Hilda's husband and sons watched the semi-trailer they were fixing to load buck and heave like a rodeo bull.

Measuring 7.3 on the Richter Scale, the Borah Peak Earthquake lasted about seven seconds. In Thousand Springs Valley, just below Idaho's tallest peak, the ground under the Smith ranch sank nine feet, while Mount Borah grew twelve inches. Two miles from Wiley's breakfast table, the land ripped, forming an escarpment twenty-one miles long and in many places six feet high.

In Challis, two children were crushed by a falling building. Shock waves raced through the earth's crust, rattling windows 500 miles from the epicenter. For a couple of hours after the quake, water spouted from Chilly Butte near Wiley's ranch, and the Mackay Reservoir bubbled like a caldron. On the valley floor, sand boils created dwarf craters, and 400 billion gallons of water poured forth from new springs. A year later, Parsons Creek on the Goddard property was still flowing two feet above normal.

In southern Idaho, seismic events such as the Borah Peak Earthquake have been going on for seventeen million years. Known by geologists as "Basin and Range faulting," these tremors have inched from west to east across the state, erecting mountain chains such as the White Knobs and Lost Rivers.

Idaho sits in the northern part of the Basin and Range Province, which had its genesis in southeastern Oregon and now extends into Mexico and eastern Idaho. The entire province includes over 150 mountain ranges and their defining valleys. They run generally north-south.

North America's Basin and Range structure is caused by forces within the earth's mantle that are slowly stretching and thinning the crust. The distance between the Atlantic and Pacific seaboards is increasing at one-half inch per year even as the North American plate drifts toward Hawaii. Valleys such as Thousand Springs are growing wider, while the mountains towering above them are pushing toward the clouds.

This mountain building occurs because the upper rocks in the North American plate's western crust are being split into enormous blocks. These brittle, sub-sur-face blocks—some a dozen or more miles thick—ride on slippery, puttylike rocks that float on the earth's mantle. The breaks among the blocks are known as faults, and it's along these that the blocks slide.

The earth's 2,000-mile-thick mantle behaves like a

**Borah Peak Earthquake Escarpment knifing along the base of
the Big Lost River Mountains.**

liquid, although it is solid. Its extremely high temperature keeps it viscous, and pressure from the buoyant crust prevents it from melting. Heat causes the rocks closest to the mantle to take on its malleable properties.

As an analogy, imagine a large chunk of marble resting atop a thick rubber sheet that floats in a vat of hot saltwater taffy. Consider the marble being sawed into domino-size pieces, each cut at an angle of sixty degrees. If opposite sides of the sheet are then pulled, the stretching rubber will widen the spaces among the dominoes. As they topple against one another, their higher, leading edges will form miniature mountain ridges, while the spaces between them become tiny valleys.

On a bigger scale, as the rocks beneath southern Idaho are broken into blocks by the stretching crust, they tilt, forming mountain ranges and basins. Gravity, rain and streams erode the peaks, bringing down detritus and filling the valley floors with sediment. This added weight unbalances the blocks even more, further sinking the valleys, while lifting the mountains.

A similar thing happens when weight is shifted to a new position on a floating air mattress. The area under the added weight sags, while that losing weight rises. Of course in the real world, the erosion occurs over tens of thousands of years. Its deposits slowly build up pressure on the unstable blocks, which is periodically released in a few heart-stopping seconds.

Just as Basin and Range faulting has widened the distance from Boise to Idaho Falls, it's now working to pull Victor away from Pocatello. In the future, eastern Idaho will continue to experience earthquakes such as the one that shook the Goddard and Smith households during the autumn of 1983.

* * * * *

Borah Peak Earthquake Escarpment Interpretive
Site: From Arco drive north on US 93. The highway follows the Big Lost River Valley, which was formed by the
same Basin and Range faulting that built the Lost River
and White Knob mountains on either side. Approximately
22 miles north of Mackay (32 miles south of Challis for
those coming from the north), turn right (northeast) on
Doublesprings Pass Road; the interpretive site is 2 miles
beyond. This non-fee area has picnic tables and convenience facilities.

The clearly-visible scarp runs along the base of the
Lost River Range. Continue driving up the Doublesprings
Pass Road for stunning views of Borah Peak (at 12,662
feet, Idaho's highest point) and Thousands Springs Valley.

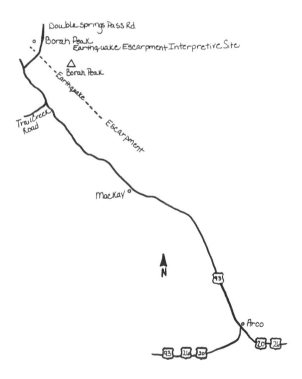

5

FIRE ABOVE,
WATER BELOW

Covering an area a little larger than Maryland, the lava fields of Idaho's eastern Snake River Plain testify to the volcanic forces that shaped our state. For eons magma spurted and oozed from the nearly 1,000 inconspicuous shield volcanoes that dot the Plain's tortured contours. As recently as 2,100 years ago titanium-rich Blue Dragon lava spewed from the fissures of Craters of the Moon National Monument. Even underlying the Plain's patchwork farms, lush with potato plants and hay, is a bed of basalt.

When you're driving past the blackened buttes, cinder cones and collapsed lava tubes, it is easy to imagine a time when Idaho ran orange with fire and molten rock.

Bouncing along any one of the eastern Snake River Plain's many back roads gives a sense of how uncompromising this country really is. Although the lava no longer flows, its imprint is everywhere. Away from the hardened magma, the sun works in harmony with the desert sands, begrudging the sagebrush and wheatgrass for the scantiest drop of moisture.

In this arid landscape who would think that below the surface lies enough water to cover all of Idaho to a

Aa lava sculptures at
Craters of the Moon
National Monument.

Twisted tree and
wildflowers amid the
lava at Craters of the
Moon National
Monument.

depth of four feet? Layers of porous basalt, some over a mile thick, soak up water like a sponge. Rivers such as the Big Lost carry snowmelt from the peaks to the upper Snake River Plain. Near Howe, that stream seeps into the Snake River Plain Aquifer. Percolating through the pervious rock, the water traverses nearly 100 miles before gushing to daylight at Thousand Springs. Trickling through the aquifer at two to ten feet per day, water that we now see issuing from Niagara Springs fell as snow in the Boulder Mountains when Thomas Jefferson was a boy.

It would take fifty-nine American Falls Reservoirs to equal the amount of water in the top 100 feet of the aquifer. If completely drained, it would fill Lake Erie. Although the aquifer's upper reaches are the most permeable, in places it may be 5,500 feet deep.

Since Julion "Duke" Clawson first drilled into the

Niagara Springs—the largest of Idaho's Thousand Springs.

aquifer a little north of Rupert in 1947, its waters have greened vast acres of desert loess. Several thousand wells now tap its liquid treasure, providing sustenance to over 130,000 Idahoans.

Before irrigated farming, the aquifer obtained its water from streams such as the Big Lost River and from the eight to fourteen inches of annual precipitation that soak into the plain. As more and more rangeland has been cultivated, water from canal irrigation has become the aquifer's principal replenishing source.

Since the mid-1950s, when the aquifer was at its fullest, farmers have learned to irrigate more efficiently. The wide use of sprinklers means less water is available to seep into the ground. In some places the aquifer is fifteen percent lower than it was just forty years ago. However, it still holds more than it did in 1900.

*　*　*　*　*

CRATERS OF THE MOON NATIONAL MONUMENT: Located on US 20/26/93, 19 miles southwest of Arco and 25 miles northeast of Carey. Except for certain winter holidays, the visitor center is open year-round.

Established by President Coolidge in 1924, this 83-square-mile volcanic landmark began erupting 15,000 years ago and has continued doing so at 2,000-year intervals. The visitor center offers informative displays as well as a film showing how the Monument's cinder cones, lava tubes and spatter cones were formed. A 7-mile loop road leads past Pahoehoe (pronounced pa-hoy-hoy) and Aa (ah-ah) lava flows. The Hawaiian name "Pahoehoe" is an apt description for this lava type. Its smooth, blue-sheen rolls do resemble "ropy coils." Aa lava derives its name not from its looks, but from how it feels. After walking for several minutes over an ankle-twisting, Vibram-sole-eating stretch of Aa, you're sure to agree that it's "hard on the feet." It's easy to imagine the cries uttered by the first native to venture barefoot onto this crusted rubble: "Ahh! Ahh!"

Fortunately, the National Park Service has built trails throughout the Monument. Visitors can explore Dewdrop, Surprise and Beauty caves or search for "lava bombs"— molten dollops that were hurled high in the air, then cooled and hardened as they tumbled to the ground— while hiking across Trench Mortar Flat.

Although it may seem difficult to believe, this inhospitable land is home to 148 types of birds, 47 species of mammals and 8 classes of reptiles. If you're lucky, you might see a bobcat slinking alongside Broken Top or a prairie falcon riding the air currents above Half Cone. Over 200 plant varieties, including bitterbrush, mock orange and tansybush, thrive among the crevices and cinders. In late spring and early summer, wildflowers paint the dark contours with blues and yellows and reds.

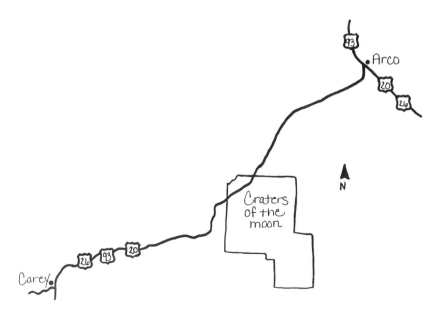

NIAGARA SPRINGS (largest of the Snake River's Thousand Springs): From I-84 Exit 157 near Wendell, drive south 7.8 miles on Orchard Valley Road. The springs are located 0.1 mile past the Niagara Springs Steelhead Hatchery.

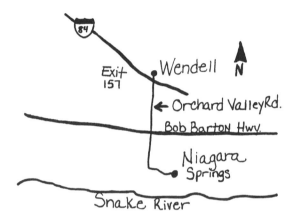

6

From Fire to Ice:
The Shoshone Indian Ice Caves

During the 1890s, summer visitors to Shoshone, Idaho, often wilted when stepping down from the passenger coaches of the Oregon Short Line Railroad. The temperature in August and early September frequently tipped 100°. Imagine their surprise when these travelers walked into one of the town's twenty-two saloons and were offered iced beer.

For countless ages before the white man ever set foot on the Snake River Plain, the Shoshone Indians and their prehistoric relatives knew about an ice cave just south of Black Butte (thirty-eight miles south of Sun Valley, near the Magic Reservoir). Each year during their migration to the camas fields below the Soldier Mountains, the Indians tarried by the cave for a few days.

Legend says that the Evil Spirit of Darkness lured Edahow, the Shoshone Princess of Light and Fertility, into the cave and imprisoned her in an icy tomb. The tribe awaited the time when the ice would melt, once more allowing Edahow to nurture the People of the Snake.

In 1884, ten-year-old Alfa Kinsey was herding his father's sheep across the lava-buckled plain beside Black

Butte, when he "discovered" a cave filled with ice. Soon, some resourceful businessmen from the nearby hamlet of Shoshone began harvesting the ice and freighting it by wagon to the town's saloons and restaurants. The enterprise folded in 1900 after excavating over 50,000 cubic feet of ice from the cave.

Ten years later, spelunkers slithered into a second chamber, where they encountered more ice. After reaching a third and final chamber, they found it plugged with an ice slab measuring twenty-one feet high by thirty-eight feet wide.

With the front cave no longer being quarried, the ice grew until eventually threatening to choke it shut. Then in 1930, the entrance was enlarged to afford easier passage. This ill-considered "enhancement" allowed the warmer outside air to invade the caves. The ice slowly, but steadily, began to melt.

In 1936, the caves came under the auspices of the Federal Government's Works Progress Administration (WPA), which added amenities making the three caverns more accessible to the public. By the following year, the large ice block in the last chamber had lost one-third of its volume.

That winter when the caves were left unattended, vandals skirted the receding ice wall and dynamited a hole in the rear chamber. Now having two entrances, the sweltering summer air funneled through the caves with a vengeance. Within five years the ice was only a memory.

The Shoshone Indian Ice Caves had their genesis during an eruption of Black Butte, one of the many shield volcanoes dotting the Snake River Plain. A river of basalt lava oozed from the crater, flowing like molasses on a frosty morning.

The molten stream meandered south, following the land's dips and gullies. As it sluggishly seared a path across the countryside, this tide of hot viscous rock cooled at its surface while its orange center remained in flux. A crust hardened around the fiery core that was continually fed by lava spewing from Black Butte. When the volcano eventually exhausted its reservoir of magma, the fluid rock emptied out of its basalt tunnel, leaving a hollow tube many miles long.

Tourist entering the Shoshone Indian Ice Caves.

As the lava tube aged, parts of its roof collapsed, forming rubble-strewn sinkholes and sealing the remaining sections of the tube into caverns, some nearly fifty feet tall. A couple of miles south of Black Butte, two portions of the tube crumpled, enclosing between them three vaulted chambers. Then in the eastern-most chamber, a bit of the ceiling toppled, opening a small hole.

For countless winters, dense, cold air sank through this hole, displacing the warmer air. During Idaho's torrid summers, the hot outside air remained above the caves, unable to penetrate the heavier, frigid air within. Water seeping into the Shoshone Indian Ice Caves froze, in time nearly filling the three caverns with ice. The caves behaved like a "natural refrigerator" until modern man altered their configuration.

From 1941 until the mid-1950s, the damaged Shoshone Indian Ice Caves sat vacant. Then Russell Robinson took over their management and began to experiment, hoping to get the ice to reform. He patched the rear hole blasted by vandals twenty years before, and reduced the size of the front entrance. To his delight, the ice reappeared.

Today, the 1,700-foot-long Shoshone Indian Ice Caves have an ice floor that varies from eight to thirty feet thick. An electric pump removes fifty gallons of water per day from the caves. If it didn't, four feet of new ice would accumulate each year, eventually filling the caves to their arched ceilings.

* * * * *

SHOSHONE INDIAN ICE CAVES: Located along State Highway 75, 17 miles north of Shoshone (12 miles south of the US 20-State Highway 75 intersection). Guided tours are available May through September. Mailing address:

1561 Highway 75 North, Shoshone, ID 83352. The caves are cold, even in the summer, so be sure to take a jacket or sweater.

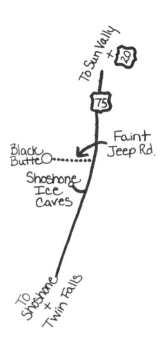

BLACK BUTTE: The broken summit sits 1 mile west of State Highway 75 and is clearly visible from the road. An unmarked jeep trail 1.2 miles north of the turnoff to the ice caves leads to the volcano's rim. High clearance vehicles only.

Black Butte—lava source for the Shoshone Indian Ice Caves.

7

MENAN BUTTES

About twenty miles north of Idaho Falls, Henry's Fork and the Snake River converge. The Menan Buttes loom over this confluence as though they were petrified mounds of Rocky Road ice cream. A close inspection of these twin volcanoes reveals a composite of brown tuff intermixed with white quartzite pebbles, much like a chocolate sundae laden with marshmallows.

Thirty thousand years ago, Henry's Fork and the Snake merged a mile or so northwest of where they do now. For countless ages these rivers had deposited gravel, clay, sand and silt at their junction, forming a thick alluvial fan that was saturated by snowmelt floods each spring. Hundreds of feet beneath this moist delta sat the Snake River Plain Aquifer, with its many layers of water-permeated basalt.

Across southeastern Idaho, internal forces stretched the earth's skin, creating rifts. In the country north and south of the Snake River Plain, this "Basin and Range faulting," as the geologists call it, continued nudging up the Lost River Mountains, the Portneufs and their sister peaks.

On the Snake River Plain, lava oozed from splits such
as the Great Rift and from the numerous shield volcanoes
that dotted the landscape. Flowing slowly like cold syrup
on a January morning, each new eruption smothered the
plain with yet another porous blanket of black basalt.

Below the Henry's Fork–Snake River delta, the continental crust fractured, allowing magma to begin rising
toward the surface. Pressured by heat from the earth's
mantle, the liquid basalt welled from its reservoir, sluicing
through the cracks as though they were a subterranean
pipeline.

Striking first the aquifer and then the sodden flood-
plain, the red-hot magma flashed the water into a mighty
steam explosion. Along a three-mile fissure, massive
clouds of basalt cinders, river rock and ash burst into the
sky. As the heavier rubble rained back to earth, it started
building two rings of tuff around the spewing craters.

Wave after wave of magma surged forth, vaporizing
the groundwater into billowing clouds. The continual
wind pushed the clouds northeast, where the settling ash
eventually added elliptical aprons to the growing buttes.

Even by modern measures of time, the eruptions
lasted but a short while, a few months at most. In their
wake stood two volcanic cones, one 500, the other 800 feet
tall, with 300-foot-deep craters marking their center
vents.

Because the Menan Buttes blocked its channel,
Henry's Fork carved a new one farther east, while its confluence with the Snake migrated south. Their combined
currents also dredged a fresh riverbed, which today skirts
around the southern butte's lower end.

* * * * *

Contoured hayfield at the foot of North Menan Butte.

MENAN BUTTES: A National Natural Landmark. From
I-15 Exit 143, drive east 12 miles on State Highway 33, or
from the Rexburg Exit of US 20, drive west 7.4 miles on
State Highway 33; turn south at the Sportsman Access for
the Menan Buttes and drive 4.1 miles as the road climbs
over the saddle between the two buttes. To hike up the
higher northern butte, turn right on the unmarked, steep
dirt road leading 0.2 miles to a parking area. An easy
(although sometimes obscure) trail leads to the rim; if you
miss it, it's possible to scramble up from almost anywhere.
Before hiking into the crater or around the rim, take your
bearings so you'll know where to descend to your car. The
view of Henry's Fork and the Snake River Plain is well
worth the effort. Approaches to the south butte cross private land; request permission before hiking.

From the
north butte dirt
road turnoff,
continue 0.8
miles to Twin
Buttes Road. Go
left for access to
the Snake River.
To return to
State Highway
33, turn right
and drive 4
miles to an
unnamed inter-
section; turn
left and proceed
another 1.1
miles.

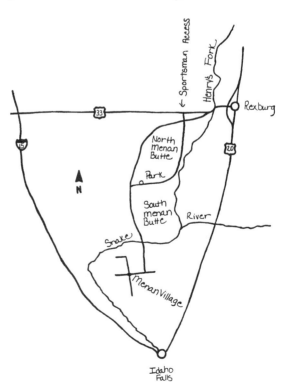

8

The Spokane Floods

Where the Clark Fork River enters the eastern border of northern Idaho, Cabinet Gorge pinches the current into a narrow channel before letting it empty into Lake Pend Oreille. During the most recent ice age, glaciers inching down from Canada cloaked Idaho's panhandle beneath a white mantle. A bit upstream from the mouth of the Clark Fork, the compressed snow piled over a mile high, plugging the river at Cabinet Gorge. Behind it, meltwater from Montana's glaciers formed the greatest ice-dammed lake ever recorded: Glacial Lake Missoula.

Eventually growing to the equivalent of three Rhode Islands, the lake's 500 cubic miles of water lapped at its glacial stopper. Then somewhere around 20,000 years ago, Lake Missoula gnawed away the edges of its frozen dam.

The lighter, less dense ice popped out of the gorge like a champagne cork. With nothing to hold it back, a mountain of water nearly 1.7 times as tall as the Empire State Building surged over Sandpoint, down the Purcell Trench toward Coeur d'Alene and westward into Washington's Spokane River Valley.

Boulders as big as school buses were carried for hun-

dreds of miles aboard iceberg rafts hurled like surfboards
before a giant wave. In eastern Washington, the torrent
fanned over the countryside and scraped the earth to its
basalt core. Today, a barren scabland the size of Delaware
offers silent testimony to the flood's power.

Striking the lower Snake, the cataclysm reversed the
river's course. Yielding to the inland tide, the Snake
recoiled, its current racing back upstream until it was once
more in Idaho. At the state line, the surge divided, one
part turning south to drive the Snake almost to within
sight of Hells Canyon, while the other slammed into the
Clearwater. When the upriver momentum finally
exhausted its energy, the lowlands where Lewiston now
stands lay under 600 feet of water. Today, the city rests on
a terrace of sediment left behind when the flood receded.

During the flood's one- or two-day climax, the flow

Clark Fork River squeezed by the cliffs of Cabinet Gorge.

reached that of 2,300 Columbia Rivers. Within a few weeks, the equal of sixty-two Lake Meads scoured northern Idaho and the Columbia Plateau before filling the Columbia River Gorge and then submerging what are now Portland, Oregon, and the Willamette Valley.

Eventually, the water drained into the Pacific Ocean, but in its wake lay potholes, gravel bars, canyons and the scars of dead waterfalls. Idaho's Lake Coeur d'Alene and Priest Lake owe their existence to the Spokane Floods.

Yes, floods. After the initial one, glaciers again choked Cabinet Gorge, allowing Lake Missoula to refill. Once more the ice cork popped and the cataract roared across the Idaho panhandle and on to the sea.

Geologists have counted forty-one separate floods, each progressively smaller than the first one, which was 25,000 times larger than any ever recorded on the Mississippi River. That Spokane Flood was perhaps the greatest flood in the history of the world.

* * * * *

CABINET GORGE: Drive State Highway 200, 30 miles east from Sandpoint, turning right at the sign for the Cabinet Gorge Dam Overlook. For much of the way, the road parallels picturesque Lake Pend Oreille, Idaho's largest lake.

Fur trappers named Cabinet Gorge after the many nooks eroded in its canyon walls. In the early 1920s, the Board on Geographic Names chose Clark Fork (in honor of William Clark) for the river over names it had been known by in the past, such as Hell Gate, Silverbow, and Missoula. Completed in 1952, Cabinet Gorge Dam holds back the Clark Fork River in a 24-mile-long reservoir, nearly all of which is in Montana.

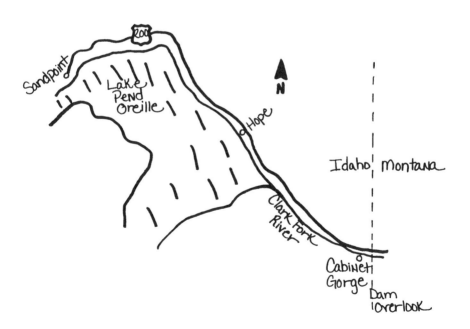

9

THE SNAKE:
A MIGHTY RIVER WITH MANY NAMES

In 1805 when William Clark reached the lower Snake River near present-day Lewiston, Idaho, he assumed that it and the Salmon were one and the same. Indians had told him about a major river merging with the Salmon from the south, but Clark thought it was merely a tributary. Because he had already honored Meriwether Lewis, the co-commander of their Voyage of Discovery, by naming the Salmon after him, Clark applied Lewis's name to the lower Snake as well. Early nineteenth century cartographers eventually corrected Clark's mistake, designating the Snake River as the "Lewis Fork of the Columbia" and the Salmon as the "North Branch of the Lewis."

When the Astorian Wilson Price Hunt saw the South Fork of the Snake in 1811, he dubbed it the "Canoe River." Upon reaching the Snake's North Fork, Hunt christened it "Henry's Fork," for Andrew Henry, who had wintered beside it several months before. After Hunt's men abandoned their boat-descent of the Snake at the falls of Caldron Linn, they labeled it the "Mad River." "Henry's Fork" was the only name that stuck.

Collectively, the Shoshones called themselves

"Neme" or people. Their sign was the snake, and they used its writhing motion to greet strangers. Some bands named their majestic river "Biavahünu" (large water trench), while others called it "Pohogawa," meaning River of the Sage Plain. Fur trappers like William Sublette and Jedediah Smith referred to the Shoshones as the "Snake Indians" and substituted "Snake River" for "Lewis Fork of the Columbia."

After gazing at the farms of Magic Valley, made green by the Snake's liquid treasure, a few modern writers have tagged the river the "Nile of Idaho."

By whatever name, the Snake River owes its existence to the ice ages. Although Idaho shows evidence of only two glacial periods, some geologists think the state may have undergone over a dozen. While the latest one reached its zenith 15,000 years ago, the first may have formed two or three million years earlier.

During each of the ice ages, glaciers blanketed the state's panhandle and sculpted the mountains into jagged pinnacles. On the Snake River Plain, the heavy winter snows melted during the brief, rainy summers. In the warm, interglacial periods, the ice thawed, releasing vast torrents. Valleys, such as Swan and Teton, saw the runoff erode new streambeds as it raced relentlessly downhill.

On the eastern Snake River Plain, the water searched out the low ground, where the south-sloping basalt landscape disappeared under the north-reaching alluvial deposits from mountain ranges like the Portneufs and Albions. Because the Snake River Plain also dropped elevation from east to west, the water rushed toward present-day Mountain Home and Boise, where it pooled in a chain of vast lakes, known collectively as Lake Idaho.

During this time, one of the lake's outlets was a minor branch of the Salmon River. This predecessor of the Snake began eroding its way upstream, eventually eating through

Lake Idaho's northern rim. About one million years ago, the lake gushed from its boundary, enlarging the Snake's channel as it drained and carving Hells Canyon.

With each succeeding ice age, the Snake cut ever deeper. By the end of the most recent one, 10,000 years ago, the Snake had become a mighty river.

Today, the Snake meanders 1,110 miles, descending over 8,500 feet from the mountains of Yellowstone National Park to the Columbia River near Kennewick, Washington. In Hells Canyon, it roils through the nation's deepest gorge, at 7,900 feet, one-third mile deeper than the Grand Canyon. From headwaters to mouth, the Snake drains 3.7 percent of the total land area of the lower forty-eight states. Rated by volume of water carried, it is America's sixth largest river; by length, her tenth longest. The Snake's annual flow could fill Hoover Dam's Lake Mead and have enough left over to flood every farm on the Snake River Plain to a depth of two feet.

Although it's 340 miles shorter than the Colorado River, the Snake carries double the amount of water. Yet each summer at Milner Dam, west of Burley, virtually the entire river is drained into the irrigation canals of Magic Valley. Then below Twin Falls, the river miraculously begins to refill, fed first by the Thousand Springs of the Snake River Plain Aquifer and later by rivers such as the Malad, Bruneau, and Boise.

The Snake has witnessed the two greatest floods the world has ever known. The first Spokane Flood, 20,000 years ago, released a wall of water across northern Idaho, creating Lake Coeur d'Alene before washing away eastern Washington's topsoil. Striking the Snake at its mouth, this surge raced upstream, reversing the river's course and depositing an island of sediment on which Lewiston now stands.

Then 14,500 years ago, the top 300 feet of ancient

Lake Bonneville hurdled through the Snake's gorges, in some places leaving gravel flats such as the ones Burley and Rupert are built on and in others eroding alcoves like the Blue Lakes Complex of Twin Falls, where golfers now attempt to break par.

Modern man has sought to tame the Snake River, sectioning it with dams. Turbines at these hydroelectric facilities generate power for four states. Every summer, thousands of acres of thirsty Idaho farmland are nurtured by endless miles of irrigation ditches, all fed by the Snake. Over one-half million Idahoans—fifty percent of the state—live on the 100-mile-wide ribbon of land that straddles the Snake's channel.

Without the Snake River, southern Idaho wouldn't enjoy the bounty it has today. Still, this wealth comes at a price.

Salmon no longer spawn within sight of Shoshone Falls. Pesticide-laden silt is slowly choking the reservoirs. And between Murtaugh and Upper Salmon Falls, algae is suffocating the fish and other aquatic animals.

Dams, such as Swan Falls and Brownlee, have halted the salmon's migration, and Milner so reduces the downstream flow, the river is unable to flush its algae-breeding pollutants.

The Snake is a great river, but some Idahoans think it's being asked to do too much. Its plight has set environmentalists against farmers, rafters against jet boaters, and fishermen against the power authorities.

The Snake's problems are too complex for the quick fixes that usually favor one constituency while threatening the values or livelihood of another. There are no easy answers. Nonetheless, solutions must be found before Idaho loves the Snake River to death.

* * * * *

View from Sinker Butte:
Swan Falls Dam holding back the Snake River.

SWAN FALLS DAM (the Snake River's first dam): From I-84 Exit 44 west of Boise, drive 8 miles south on State Highway 69 to Kuna. At the Kuna Ward LDS Church where the road curves sharply right, continue straight 20 yards and turn left on Swan Falls Road. The Dam is 21 miles south in the Snake River Birds of Prey National Conservation Area. Watch for raptors gliding on the air currents and for the numerous prairie dogs, which make up their diet.

Completed in 1901 to provide hydroelectric power for the mines of nearby Silver City, the Swan Falls Dam had the unintended consequence of blocking salmon migration up the Snake River. Over the years the original structure has been upgraded several times. A fish ladder added to the dam in 1922 was poorly designed and did little to reverse the salmon's demise.

A footbridge across the dam leads to hiking and mountain biking trails. Sinker Butte (the high point south of the river; elevation 3,421 feet) offers stunning views of the Snake River Plain and Owyhee Mountains.

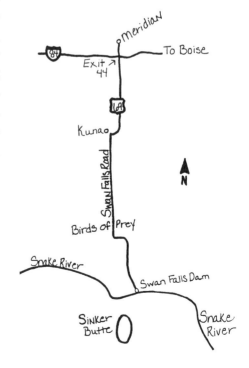

10

THE BONNEVILLE FLOOD

Imagine an ancient Native American standing on the south rim of the Snake River Canyon near present-day Twin Falls. A faint roar catches his ear. Glancing down at the river, he notices its churning waves battering the canyon's sides.

The sound amplifies, rumbling with the throaty clamor of a thunderstorm. Beneath the onlooker's feet the earth vibrates like the skin of a bass drum.

Suddenly, a surge of brown froth bursts around the distant bend, hits the outside cliff and ricochets across the chasm. Behind the foam, driving it, hurling it at break-neck speed, rushes a boiling caldron.

Striking the narrows, the water piles up, while north of the canyon another torrent barrels across the lava plain toward the rim, then plunges over in a sweeping cataract. In the gorge the river climbs the shadowed walls to the brim and overflows.

During the last ice age, Idaho's panhandle slept under a blanket of snow. Glaciers scooped 1,000 feet of sediment from Lake Pend Oreille and choked the Purcell Trench toward Rathdrum. In the Bitterroots and

Sawtooths, ice carved the mountains into precipitous pinnacles and knife-edged arêtes.

But on the Snake River Plain and in the valleys edg-
ing into Utah, the heavy winter snows melted during the
brief, rainy summers. Much of this water collected in a
vast, undrained basin called Lake Bonneville.

Spreading across 20,000 square miles of northern
Utah and eastern Nevada, Lake Bonneville eventually
stretched its fingers into southern Idaho. With no river to
siphon it off, the lake grew for 13,000 years until covering
the Salt Lake City town-site with 800 feet of water. In
Idaho, what are now the hay fields outside Franklin and
Preston lay submerged, as did I-15 east of Woodruff and
parts of the Curlew Valley.

At Red Rock Pass, the lake's lowest boundary, the
waves eventually spilled over the shoreline. For the next
five centuries Lake Bonneville held constant, its annual
accumulations drained north through a tiny, but growing,
outlet. Then in a geologic nanosecond 14,500 years ago,
the stream chewed through the stone rim into the soft
alluvium underbelly.

Water began pouring down Marsh Creek to the
Portneuf River and into the Snake. As each bit of rock and
clay eroded from its path, the deluge became a torrent,
then a flood.

In an instant the pass was sliced to bedrock, and the
top 300 feet of Lake Bonneville gushed forth. For nearly a
month during the peak discharge, the equivalent flow of
three Amazon Rivers hurdled across Idaho.

Nothing withstood the flood as it rolled and polished boulders the size of Volkswagen Bugs. Near
Massacre Rocks State Park, it flushed away a basalt dam
that had built a prehistoric lake where the American Falls
Reservoir now stands.

Above the Murtaugh narrows, the Snake River

ponded until overflowing its northern flank, then charged west, carving the Eden Channel and scraping the loess-cloaked basalt to a blackened scab. At Twin Falls these floodwaters poured back into the main canyon, forming the Blue Lakes complex.

Massive whirlpools sucked away the streambed beneath bands of hard volcanic rock, creating spectacular drops such as Shoshone Falls. Every constricted bend along the entire Snake River gorge bunched the water to overflowing. At Rock Creek, at Swan Falls, at Pittsburg Landing while the ponding flood awaited release, it deposited its burden of gravel and sand in mile-long, 100-foot-high bars such as the ones rafters now picnic on in Hells Canyon.

Car-size boulder at Massacre Rocks State Park.
Stones even larger than this were rolled and polished
by the Bonneville Flood.

Although the peak flow lasted but a few weeks, Lake Bonneville continued draining for ten months, ultimately releasing enough water to fill Lake Michigan.

Centuries later when the glaciers melted, the lake's residue began evaporating. Today, the Great Salt Lake is all that remains. Should the world undergo another ice age, Lake Bonneville could once more resurge. Yet without the eroded lip of Red Rock Pass, it will never again attain its former majesty.

* * * * *

MASSACRE ROCKS STATE PARK: Located on the strip of land between I-86 and the Snake River, 10 miles southwest of American Falls. The park is open year-round, the visitor center from Memorial Day weekend through Labor Day; non-reservation camping. Mailing address: 3592 N. Park Lane, American Falls, ID 83211.

As you walk among the boulder fields dotting the park, observe how the rocks have been rounded and polished. Try to imagine the volume of water needed to roll boulders the size of minivans.

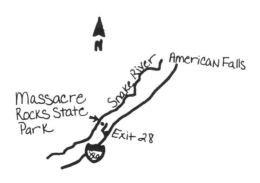

PERRINE BRIDGE SNAKE RIVER OVERLOOK: Located 0.5 miles north of Twin Falls on US 93. Walkways along the bridge as well as overlooks on both sides of the river provide stunning views of the Blue Lakes cataract complex, which was formed during the Bonneville Flood.

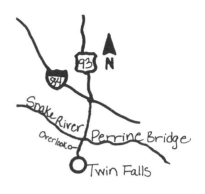

Perrine Bridge shadow on the Snake River where the waters of the Bonneville Flood once filled the canyon to the brim.

RED ROCK PASS: From I-15 Exit 36 between Pocatello and the Utah state line, drive south 12 miles on US 91. The pass is marked by a state interpretive sign. While there, look along the Bannock and Portneuf foothills that delineate Marsh Valley. In some places you can see the faint waterlines left by ancient Lake Bonneville.

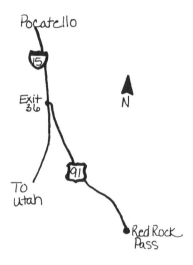

A People
Forged by
Courage

11

SACAJAWEA'S IDAHO HOMECOMING

In early August, 1805, the Voyage of Discovery was in its second year. Captains Meriwether Lewis and William Clark had already explored the Missouri River to the Three Forks. Now as their men laboriously dragged their canoes through the rocky shallows of the Beaverhead River (north of Dillon, Montana), the captains looked forward to reaching the Missouri's headwaters and cresting the Continental Divide.

On August 8, as the expedition set up its evening camp, Sacajawea, the Shoshone wife of the interpreter Charbonneau, excitedly pointed at a distant hill, calling it the "Beaver's Head." She remembered it from her childhood, before her capture by a Hidatsa war party. She said her people spent their summers in a valley to the west. Motioning toward the Beaverhead Mountains, she told Lewis and Clark about a pass the Shoshones used when going to hunt buffalo. She felt certain her tribe was somewhere beyond.

Lewis and Clark knew they must find Indians. The expedition had to have horses, or it would be unable to transport its supplies over the mountains.

The following morning, Lewis and three other men left the main party, intending to cross the Bitterroot Range and locate the Shoshones. Clark was to continue up the Beaverhead River with the expedition's canoes.

On August 12, Lewis climbed Lemhi Pass and entered Idaho. That afternoon, he had his first drink from a creek whose waters eventually flowed to the Pacific Ocean.

The next day, Lewis descended into the Lemhi Valley. Although he spotted several Indians, they ran off when he tried to approach. Heading north along the Lemhi River, he finally came on three women who didn't flee. Lewis gave the women presents, persuading them to lead him to their home. They took him two miles farther when sixty Shoshone warriors came galloping to the women's rescue.

After learning that the women were unharmed, Chief Cameahwait invited the Americans to the Shoshones' camp (near Tendoy). Lewis soon prevailed upon the chief and some of his band to accompany him back over Lemhi Pass to where Clark and the rest of the party were waiting. As an added inducement, Lewis said the expedition contained a young Shoshone woman who'd been taken captive as a girl.

When the Shoshones reached the Americans' main body, Sacajawea began sucking her fingers, a sign that the Indians were members of her tribe. To her immense joy, she discovered a woman with whom she'd been friends as a child. The Hidatsas had stolen them at the same time, and Sacajawea's friend had escaped by leaping through a stream.

While the two women renewed their bond, Lewis and Clark began to parley with Chief Cameahwait. After smoking a ceremonial pipe, the captains sent for Sacajawea. When she entered the tent where they were

Agency Creek Road winding its way down from Lemhi Pass.

meeting, she recognized the chief as her brother. Overcome by her emotions, the young woman embraced him while weeping tears of happiness.

During the next three days, Captain Clark, Sacajawea, Charbonneau, and eleven other members of the expedition accompanied the Shoshones over Lemhi Pass to their camp in the Lemhi Valley. Taking a native guide, Clark continued to the Salmon River, hoping it would provide a water passage to the coast. He was soon disappointed. Several miles west of present-day North Fork, he judged the Salmon unrunable, deeming it a "river of no return."

Meanwhile at the Shoshones' camp, Sacajawea met a warrior to whom as a girl she'd been promised in marriage. To her relief, the brave renounced his claim because she had borne Charbonneau a son.

Escorted by fifty mounted Shoshones, Sacajawea and
Charbonneau re-crossed Lemhi Pass into Montana, where
the expedition was caching its canoes and surplus stores.
After ordering the remaining baggage packed on the
Indians' ponies, Lewis led the Voyage of Discovery into
Idaho to join up with Clark. On August 26, Sacajawea
topped Lemhi Pass for the last time.

* * * * *

LEMHI PASS (7,339 ft.): A National Historic Landmark
and part of the Lewis and Clark National Back Country
Byway. From Tendoy on State Highway 28 (20 miles south
of Salmon and 140 miles northwest of Idaho Falls) turn
east on Agency Creek Road for 0.1 mile. At the T, turn left

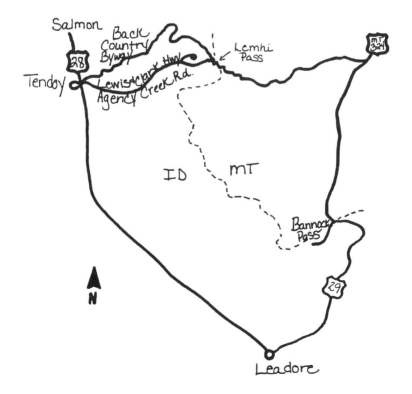

and follow the Back Country Byway signs 27 miles to Lemhi Pass. From the pass, it's 0.2 miles to the Sacajawea Memorial Campground (tents only) and the Laura Tolman Wild Flower Trail. To return to State Highway 28, descend Agency Creek Road 12.2 miles to Tendoy; along the way watch for the historical sign marking where on August 12, 1805, Meriwether Lewis spent his first night in Idaho. While these gravel roads are suitable for automobiles, trailers and buses are not advised. The roads are usually closed by snow from November to June.

BEAVERHEAD MOUNTAINS SCENIC LOOP: From Lemhi Pass follow Montana Forest Road 324 east 12.1 miles to Montana State Highway 324. Turn right and in 12.3 miles cross Bannock Pass (7,485 ft.), where the road becomes Idaho State Highway 29. Descend 13.8 miles to State Highway 28 in Leadore.

12

DAVID THOMPSON:
THE PERIPATETIC MAP MAKER

Almost blind, old David Thompson was so broke that he sold his surveying instruments and even his heavy winter coat. Several years before, he had tried selling the story of his adventures to Washington Irving, but the noted American writer and he couldn't come to terms. Then on February 16, 1857, just outside Montreal, Quebec, David Thompson died: a forgotten pauper.

Yet in his lifetime, Thompson had discovered the headwaters of the Mississippi River. He made the first complete reconnaissance of the Columbia. He surveyed much of the western boundary between the United States and Canada. He wrote thirty-nine journals and drew countless maps. And as chief topographer of the North West Company of Montreal, he rode, canoed and walked nearly 55,000 miles, many of them in Idaho.

Fourteen years old in 1784 when he sailed from England to Canada, Thompson had already been apprenticed to the Hudson's Bay Company. For thirteen years, the young Welshman worked at various posts, learning the fur trade and surveying. Finding that his interests lay in geography instead of commerce, Thompson grew restless when the company sought to discourage him from drawing maps.

In 1797 Thompson quit the Hudson's Bay Company and joined its chief rival, the North West Company. During the next fifteen years, he busied himself sorting out the tangled rivers that drained a vast fur empire. One by one the blank sections on the company's maps began to disappear.

Thompson didn't confine his curiosity to surveys. Little in the natural world escaped his interest, whether the constellations, birds, or the mosquitoes he allowed to feed on his arm while he examined their behavior through a magnifying glass. One winter he even deduced that the color of a person's eyes determined his sensitivity to snow blindness.

A religious man, Thompson forswore tobacco, profanity and whiskey. At evening campfires he often read the Bible in French to his voyageurs. And he worked tirelessly to prevent his traders from giving liquor to the Indians.

In 1808 Thompson first set foot in Idaho, coming down the Kootenai River. In September of the following year, he established Kullyspell House on a jut of land in Lake Pend Oreille. Intended for the Colville, Spokane, Coeur d'Alene, and Flathead Indian trade, this single-room log post lasted but one year until harassment by Blackfoot war parties closed its doors. Although owned by a Canadian company, Kullyspell House was the first trading post in Idaho.

During 1811-12 Thompson's explorations culminated in the first complete survey of the Columbia River. Not only mapping it from source to mouth, he also charted many of its tributaries. Side surveys took him fifty-six miles up the Snake as well as along the banks of the Clark Fork and Pend Oreille rivers.

Thompson last came through Idaho in early spring 1812 on his way to Quebec. Soon after reaching Montreal, he resigned from the North West Company. Although he continued working as a surveyor, his fortunes steadily declined until his death.

Thompson's maps remain his crowning achievement. One, measuring ten feet long, displayed the one and one-half million square miles he had explored. Considered too valuable to be seen by the North West Company's competitors, it hung in a locked room at Fort William (on the north shore of Lake Superior), visible to no one except the company's partners.

Memorial to one of North America's greatest cartographers: David Thompson.

* * * * *

DAVID THOMPSON'S MEMORIAL: Drive east from Sandpoint 16 miles on State Highway 200, turning north (left) at the sign for Hope. Follow this road through Hope for 1.2 miles; the monument is on the right, just inside East Hope.

Kullyspell House was located on Memaloose Point, a small peninsula in Lake Pend Oreille, just off Idaho State Highway 200 near Hope. According to locals, the actual site has been under water for years, ever since dams raised the elevation of the lake.

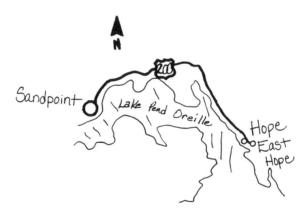

13

FORT HENRY

The Bonneville Museum in downtown Idaho Falls displays a curious rock that's chiseled with five names, a cross and the date "1810." The top name is "A. Henry."

In 1917 Hazen Hawkes uncovered this rock on his family's farm alongside Conant Creek, several miles southeast of Marysville. The location was the site of Camp Henry.

Andrew Henry had come west from St. Louis in 1809, co-commanding a Missouri Fur Company trapping brigade. Where the Madison, Jefferson and Gallatin rivers converge—the Three Forks of the Missouri—he and his mountain men built a fort and started emptying the streams of beaver. Just when they began to enjoy a bountiful harvest, the Blackfeet descended.

By June, 1810, Henry had read over eight graves, including that of George Drouillard, who first saw this country with Lewis and Clark.

Unable to fight the Blackfeet and take fur too, Henry abandoned the Three Forks but not the mountains. Near the Madison's headwaters, he and a handful of volunteers crossed the Continental Divide into Idaho. A few nights later while camped beside what is now Henry's Lake, he learned that he hadn't left his Indian problems in Montana. A party of Crows stole most of his company's horses.

With their gear packed on the few remaining mounts, the trappers trudged south, following a fork of the Snake River that within another year would also carry Henry's name. On the Egin Bench north of present-day Rexburg, half the men refused to go farther. Henry had no choice but to leave them, advising them to construct a shelter for the coming winter. Their intended quarters proved inauspicious, since "egin" is the Shoshone word for "cold."

Taking Hoback, Cather, McBride and Jackson, Andrew Henry headed up the Falls River, then turned onto Conant Creek. At what would eventually become the Hawkes's farm, the five men established Camp Henry, and one of them carved their names in a stone marker.

By the time the ice ended the trapping season, the small company had collected a good catch of pelts. Shortly after the New Year, everyone gathered on Egin Bench to wait out the snow. The men Henry left there the previous fall had built a few crude log huts.

Winter proved harder on spirit than body. Before the drifts from the last blizzard melted, one of the men snapped. Taking his rifle, he deserted. Although Henry often saw him watching the huts from afar, nothing could induce the crazed trapper to return.

In the spring, Henry and his men loaded their horses with forty packs of beaver and climbed back over the Divide. The deranged deserter stayed behind.

Andrew Henry led another fur brigade to the mountains in 1822, but he never again set foot in Idaho. The log cabins his men built beside Henry's Fork of the Snake River have come to be known as Fort Henry, America's first trading post west of the Continental Divide.

Broken monument marking the site of Fort Henry.

* * * * *

BONNEVILLE COUNTY MUSEUM: Located at the intersection of Elm and North Eastern avenues in Idaho Falls.

FORT HENRY SITE: Take the North Rexburg Exit off US 20, turning north on the Salem-Parker Road (also called North Salem Road and 1900 E Road). After 4.4 miles come to the defaced Fort Henry Monument 100 yards south of Henry's Fork River. The fort sat in the bottomland one-third mile east.

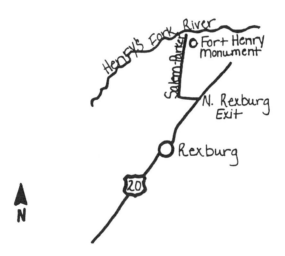

14

CALDRON LINN
AND THE ASTORIANS

In March, 1811, Wilson Price Hunt journeyed west from St. Louis, leading the Pacific Fur Company's overland expedition to Fort Astoria at the mouth of the Columbia River. Hunt was a junior partner in the company, which itself was a tiny fiefdom within John Jacob Astor's fur empire.

Astor had grand plans. He'd already dispatched the 290-ton *Tonquin* around Cape Horn to establish the Astoria trading post on the Oregon coast. Now, Hunt's sixty-two-man force was bringing the muscle to harvest the country's beaver. Trappers in Hunt's party would glean the streams and ponds of their pelts. Astor's ships would then take the furs to China, trade them for tea and silk, and sail the cargo to New York.

That autumn Hunt entered Idaho via Teton Pass. In early October his expedition reached Henry's Fork, a few miles north of present-day Rexburg. Eleven days later, the young commander left his horses with a band of Shoshones and started downriver in fifteen canoes his men had hewn from cottonwoods.

Near the Menan Buttes, where Henry's Fork converges with the South Fork of the Snake, the quicker current of the combined streams portended trouble. At American Falls, the company portaged. A bit below the future site of Milner Dam, a canoe struck a boulder and flipped, drowning Antoine Clappine. Riding with him, Ramsay Crooks, the party's deputy commander, and four others barely escaped.

A few miles later, the rowers again pulled into shore, alerted by frantic signals from the lead boat. Ahead, the river gained speed as it rushed toward a loud roar. Leaving their canoes, Hunt and his men tramped through the sagebrush that dotted the sandy bottomland.

A short distance from where they had beached, the volcanic walls pinched the Snake into a constricted flume. The bunched water shot through the gap as though sluiced down a mountain. Surging over a ledge, the river plunged into a seething basin of green frothy boils.

Caldron Linn—the southern-most point on the Snake River where lava cliffs churn the currrent into a foaming brew.

An Astorian named Robert Stuart later confided to his diary that "Hecate's caldron was never half so agitated when vomiting even the most diabolical spells, as is this Linn." From Stuart's entry, this narrowest and most southern portion of the Snake River took its name: Caldron Linn.

Wondering what other surprises the Snake might be holding, Hunt dispatched scouts. The reconnaissance cost several days and more wrecked canoes. Even worse, its conclusion was disheartening. The river wasn't navigable.

Sending Crooks and a few men to retrieve their horses from the Shoshones, Hunt waited near Caldron Linn. When some of his party asked permission to press on for Astoria on foot, the commander reluctantly allowed them to try.

Fearful lest the expedition be overtaken by winter, Crooks soon abandoned his quest for the horses and returned to Caldron Linn. Needing to move, Hunt cached everything that couldn't be carried and on November 9 began walking to the Oregon coast.

Crooks and eighteen men followed the Snake's left shore, while Hunt led the balance of the expedition down the right. For the next two months, the parties struggled across Idaho in the face of deteriorating weather. Desperately in want of food and horses, they eventually veered away from the Snake, hoping to locate friendly Indians. At the Weiser River, Hunt traded for a couple of ponies, some dried salmon, and most important, a guide.

After reuniting with Crooks' group, Hunt left the deputy leader and five others—now too exhausted to travel—in the Shoshones' care. Beyond the Snake River, the expedition headed over the Blue Mountains into the lush valleys of Oregon. For weeks on end, the weary march continued, broken only by an occasional rest with an amicable tribe.

On January 21, 1812, the company reached the Columbia River. Below The Dalles, the men again took to canoes, finally arriving at Astoria on February 15. Here, Hunt met those he had permitted to leave Caldron Linn ahead of the main body in early November. They had beat him by a month.

On May 11 Crooks, too, joined his companions at Fort Astoria, having regained his health among the Shoshones.

* * * * *

CALDRON LINN (also known as Star Falls): Drive US 30, 22 miles west from Burley or 9 miles east from Hansen, turning north toward Murtaugh on 4500 East Road. After 1.2 miles swing right into Murtaugh for another 0.4 miles. Cross the railroad tracks, go through several jogs and in 0.7 miles turn left at a T. Drive 1.6 miles, crossing the Snake River, then turn right on 1500 S and in 1 mile right again on 2000 E. In 0.7 miles come to a rough descent; walk this unless you have a four-wheel-drive, high-clearance vehicle. From the flats near the river, a short trail leads to Caldron Linn and its numerous overlooks. At the narrowest point, the gorge is but 40 feet wide. There are no handrails, so please use care.

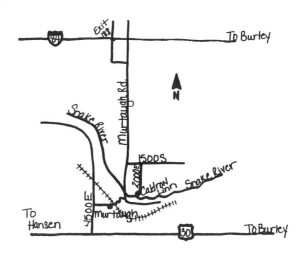

15

THE BATTLE OF PIERRE'S HOLE

"Come a runnin' boys! Indian attack! Old Milt needs your help!"

On July 18, 1832, the frenzied cry shattered the rendezvous. The mountain men's annual celebration was winding to a close in Pierre's Hole, now picturesque Teton Valley near Driggs. The horse races, shooting contests, pageantry and camaraderie had ended. During the coming months of freezing streams, hair-raising danger and mind-numbing isolation, the memory of this year's rendezvous and the anticipation of the next would be the trappers' only solace.

As the riders shouted their call to arms, the buckskin-clad men grabbed their rifles and saddles. Many blinked bloodshot eyes, attempting to rid the cobwebs from brains dulled by the river-water-diluted alcohol Bill Sublette sold as whiskey.

The day before, Henry Fraeb and Bill's brother, Milt Sublette, had moved their Rocky Mountain Fur Company brigades a few miles south, planning an early start after their trappers shed their hangovers. This morning, a couple of hours after daybreak, they encountered a large band of Gros Ventres.

Generations earlier, the Gros Ventres had migrated north to present-day Montana. Every few years since, the tribe rode south to visit its cousins, the Arapahos. In the summer of 1832, the Gros Ventres were returning home when they sighted the fur brigades.

Halting several hundred yards apart, the parties sized each other up. When a chief came forward to parley, Milt Sublette sent out Antoine Godin, who spoke the Gros Ventres' tongue, and a Flathead brave. Instead of talking, they shot the chief and lifted his scalp.

After a moment of disbelief, the Gros Ventres withdrew to a streambed and began piling deadfall and brush into a breastwork. Meanwhile, Milt Sublette sent riders to alert the rendezvous.

Pastoral Teton Basin beneath the towering Tetons,
known by the mountain men as Pierre's Hole.
During the 1832 rendezvous, the tranquillity of this
lovely valley was shattered by a deadly battle.

Soon reinforcements arrived, including Milt's brother. Seeing the trappers and allied Nez Perce and Flathead warriors milling about in an undisciplined horde, Bill Sublette took charge. He organized about thirty Indians and a like number of mountain men into an attack force and led them forward. As the makeshift army came in range of the stronghold, the Gros Ventres greeted them with a withering barrage.

Bill's fighters dove for cover and began answering the Gros Ventres' fire. All day the two sides exchanged shots. When Bill rose up for a better look, a musket ball smashed into his arm. Declining to be carried to the rear, he insisted that his men prop him against a cottonwood so he could continue directing the battle.

In the late afternoon, a Gros Ventre brave shouted that many more of his tribesmen would soon come to his aid. Within minutes a mistranslation of that threat escalated into "Hundreds of warriors are raiding the rendezvous!"

In their dash to the fight, the mountain men had left behind their Indian wives and children as well as the stores needed for the coming year. Panic quickly rolled over the brigades. Even Bill Sublette was affected.

Wheeling about like a school of jittery fish, the rattled army raced back to the rendezvous. Barely a dozen men stayed to cover the Gros Ventres. Near twilight the trappers sheepishly returned, having found camp as peaceful as a Sunday picnic.

At dawn Bill Sublette sought to renew the attack, but the Gros Ventres had crept away during the night. The Battle of Pierre's Hole was over. Five trappers and seven of their Indian allies were dead. No one knows how many casualties the Gros Ventres carried off.

* * * * *

PIERRE'S HOLE: Crossed by State Highway 33 in Teton County just west of the Wyoming state line and Teton Mountains. The 1832 rendezvous, with its trapping brigades, friendly Indian camps and grazing fields for the many horses, occupied several acres of the Teton Basin near Driggs. Although no one is certain, some historians place the battle site beside Trail Creek, 1 mile northwest of Victor.

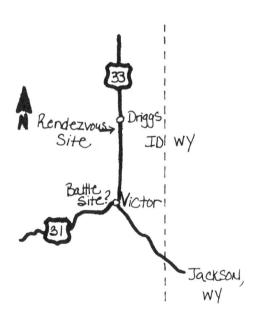

16

Fort Hall's Cambridge Ice Cutter

"Gentlemen, I will yet roll a stone into your garden that you will never be able to get out."

In June, 1834, on Ham's Fork in the southwest corner of present-day Wyoming, Nathaniel Jarvis Wyeth issued his famous threat. As the angry Wyeth strode away from Tom Fitzpatrick's and Jim Bridger's rendezvous camp, the two partners had no idea the Cambridge, Massachusetts, ice cutter would soon build a trading post in the midst of their fur empire.

Today, a small monument marks Fort Hall's location alongside the Snake River, a few miles upstream from the American Falls Reservoir. The land now belongs to the Bannock and Shoshone tribes.

Wyeth had come to the mountains two years earlier, wanting to make his fortune in beaver pelts. Compared to his previous occupation of cutting and selling ice from the pond beside his home near Harvard College, the life of a fur trader must have seemed exciting. Besides, John Jacob Astor and General William Ashley had grown rich on fur, so why not him?

Wyeth's first venture failed when the supply ship he

had sent around the Horn to meet him on the Oregon coast
sank. In 1833 he returned to Massachusetts in company
with Milt Sublette, a partner in the Rocky Mountain Fur
Company. Sublette was going east to seek medical treat-
ment for his diseased foot.

During the journey, Sublette contracted for Wyeth
to furnish the Rocky Mountain Fur Company with supplies at the next rendezvous. With that agreement in
hand, Wyeth persuaded several Boston investors to provide the financial backing.

On April 28, 1834, the Cambridge ice cutter led his
pack train west from Independence, Missouri. Milt
Sublette began the journey with him but soon turned
back; his foot had grown worse.

Wyeth drove his men and mules relentlessly as they

**Fort Hall as it looked when owned by the
Hudson's Bay Company.**

pushed along the Platte River. He needed to hurry, because hard on his heels rode Milt's brother, Bill Sublette. Bill had outfitted the Rocky Mountain Fur Company since its beginning, and he had no intention abandoning the lucrative trade to an eastern upstart. Thirteen days out from Independence, Bill Sublette's caravan edged into the lead, an advantage it never relinquished.

By the time Wyeth crossed trails with Tom Fitzpatrick's brigade on the Green River, Bill Sublette had already secured the Rocky Mountain Fur Company's trade. Fitzpatrick, the firm's managing partner, repudiated the contract Wyeth had made with Milt Sublette, leaving Wyeth stuck with several thousand dollars' worth of stores.

Instead of returning to Massachusetts with nothing to show, Wyeth decided to build a post on the Snake River and trade with the Indians. Construction began Tuesday, July 15, and was completed three weeks later. Named for one of Wyeth's investors, Henry Hall, Fort Hall became an instant thorn in the side of the Hudson's Bay Company. The British monopoly soon countered with a trading post of its own: Fort Boise.

Although Wyeth tried, he couldn't compete with the English on one side and the American fur companies on the other. Broke, he returned to his Cambridge ice business in 1836, having agreed to sell Fort Hall to the Hudson's Bay Company.

During the 1840s and early 1850s, Wyeth's former trading post became an important rest stop for thousands of families on the Oregon Trail. By the mid-1850s declining emigration and bypasses such as Hudspeth's Cutoff had so reduced the numbers of wagons passing the fort that it was no longer profitable. In 1856 the Hudson's Bay Company finally closed its gates.

* * * * *

FORT HALL REPLICA: Located in Pocatello's Ross Park. In south Pocatello, take I-15 Exit 67 to Fifth Avenue north; in 0.6 miles, turn left on Fredregill, then left again on Fourth Avenue; in 0.3 miles turn right at the sign for Upper Ross Park, Bannock County Museum and Fort Hall replica. Mailing address: P. O. Box 4169, Pocatello, ID 83205.

The old fort's actual site is in Fort Hall Bottoms near the west end of Sheepskin Road, southwest of the Fort Hall village on US 91. Since the grounds are on the reservation, visitors must secure a permit from the Shoshone-Bannock Tribal Council in Fort Hall, Idaho.

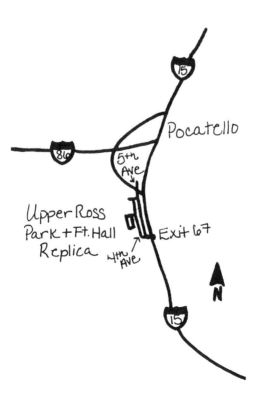

17

BENJAMIN LOUIS EULALIE DE BONNEVILLE

Bonneville County; Bonneville Peak; Bonneville Flood; Bonneville Dam; Bonneville Power Authority; Bonneville Salt Flats; the Pontiac Bonneville. . . .

"Bonneville" has been appended to much of our state and our nation. Idaho Falls has the Bonneville Museum. At Massacre Rocks State Park near American Falls are "melon" boulders, rounded and polished by the Bonneville Flood. Southeast of Pocatello stands Bonneville Peak, at 9,271 feet, the tallest point in the Portneuf Range.

Who was this man whose name not only marks so many features of the intermountain west but also embellishes a popular automobile?

Immigrant, West Point Cadet, Soldier, Fur Trapper, Patriot: During his life, Benjamin Louis Eulalie de Bonneville wore each of these titles.

He was born in France in 1796 and came to the United States as a young child. At seventeen, he won an appointment to the Military Academy and in 1815, received his commission. Bonneville's early Army career revealed little that would lead to his name being bestowed with the abandon of a politician's promises.

General B.L.E.
Bonneville.

*(Courtesy of Denver Public
Library #13689)*

Then in 1831, his superiors granted him a two-year leave to take a trapping expedition to the Rocky Mountains. Some historians speculate that he went as a spy, that he was sent to gather information about the British, who shared joint occupancy of the country we now call Washington, Oregon, Idaho, western Montana and western Wyoming. In any case, the need to arrange non-government financing for his venture and to put together the necessary provisions delayed his departure until spring, 1832.

For over three years Bonneville's trappers emptied the streams and ponds of their beaver. In Idaho, his mountain men camped beside the Bear River and the Salmon.

They also trudged across the arid Snake River Plain. Hot and thirsty when they crested a hill overlooking present-day Boise, they saw in the distance a river, its banks lush with green-leafed trees. Some legends say it was here at Bonneville Point that Bonneville's French-speaking trappers gave Idaho's capitol and its river their name: "Les bois, les bois. Voyes les bois!" ("The woods, the woods. See the woods!")

After returning to the East Coast almost two years beyond his authorized leave, Bonneville learned the Army had dropped him from its rolls. For the next twelve months while he doggedly sought reinstatement, he wrote about his western travels and eventually sold the unpolished manuscript to Washington Irving.

When the noted author rewrote and published the work as *The Adventures of Captain Bonneville,* the book

Historical marker at Bonneville Point.

became an instant success. Bonneville became a national hero, nearly on par with Lewis and Clark, his name synonymous with enterprise and daring.

Meanwhile, the Army relented and again allowed Bonneville to don a soldier's uniform. In Florida he led his troops against the Seminole Indians. During the Mexican War, he waded ashore at Vera Cruz, fought at Mexico City and was wounded by grapeshot at Churubusco. And in the 1850s, he battled the Apaches and Navahos in the southwest.

The Civil War found Bonneville too old for combat. Still, he played his part, serving as Superintendent of Recruiting in St. Louis. Shortly before Abraham Lincoln's assassination, the President signed Bonneville's promotion to Brigadier General.

On June 12, 1878, Benjamin Bonneville died. Yet through Washington Irving's pen, Bonneville's fame has lived on.

Today, as we drive past the tributes our modern world offers to his memory, we ought to take a moment to recall the man, an American patriot.

* * * * *

BONNEVILLE POINT: Take the Blacks Creek-Kuna Road Exit 64 off I-84, 9.8 miles east of Boise. Drive north on Blacks Creek Road 2.4 miles, turning left at the state historical sign; Bonneville Point is 1.4 miles beyond.

Looking west from atop this knoll during the late summer and early fall, you can see the lush green of downtown Boise. Note the contrast in colors between the land lining the Boise River and the drab brown everywhere else. Imagine yourself as one of Captain Bonneville's French trappers first seeing a ribbon of trees in full leaf after having thirsted your way across the Snake River Plain's sagebrush desert. You too might have shouted, "Les bois, les bois. Voyes les bois!"

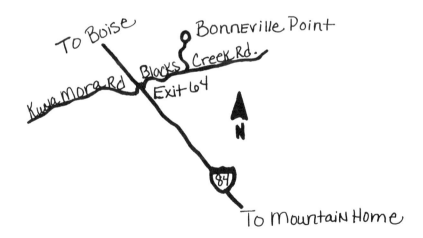

18

Ben Hudspeth's Idaho Shortcut

In mid-July, 1849, a large wagon train with 250 emigrants left the Oregon Trail at Sheep Rock, not far from Soda Springs, Idaho. Hoping to shave a week off their trip to the California goldfields, the train's leaders, Benoni Morgan Hudspeth and John J. Myers headed due west, avoiding the longer route via Fort Hall. During the subsequent years of America's great westering, thousands of pioneers used this detour, which was called Hudspeth's Cutoff.

Ben Hudspeth had grown up in Missouri, eleven miles from Independence. In the 1830s, he watched heavy freight wagons lumber past his family's farm as their teamsters began the journey along the Santa Fe Trail to New Mexico. He also saw mule trains packing supplies to the fur trappers' rendezvous and then returning some months later with their loads of beaver. In time, this northern, trappers' route became the Oregon Trail.

In the spring of 1845, Hudspeth joined John Frémont's topographical expedition to map the upper Arkansas River. Among the party's more notable members were Joe Walker and Kit Carson, men who had forged their reputations in the wilds of the Rocky Mountains. After leaving part of his force at Bent's Fort (in eastern Colorado) to complete the survey, the politically-connected Frémont headed across the Continental Divide and Great Basin into California. Among those going with him were Carson, Walker and Hudspeth.

In 1846, the United States went to war with Mexico, and Frémont seized the opportunity to precipitate California's Bear Flag Revolt. Ben Hudspeth served as an officer in Frémont's "California Battalion" until 1847, when its commander was censored by the US Government for exceeding his orders. That summer Hudspeth returned to Missouri, but the lure of California remained in his blood.

After gold was discovered near Sutter's sawmill below the Sierra Nevada Mountains, Ben Hudspeth persuaded four of his brothers to join him in a trading venture to the diggings. As pilot, he recruited John Myers, a mountain man who had also been with Frémont's expedition. Rounding out the party were emigrants willing to pay to be guided west. All together, the train numbered about forty wagons.

The Hudspeths' cargo consisted of not only shovels, picks, and gold pans, but also playing cards and liquor, goods likely to be in high demand in the rough California mining camps. Wanting to see his sons well mounted, William Hudspeth, Ben's father, gave each of them a fine thoroughbred.

On May 1, 1849, the Hudspeth wagon train rolled away from Independence. Counting oxen, mules, saddle horses and beef cattle, the train's stock totaled 600 head. Because of the experience of Ben Hudspeth and John Myers, the party reached the Bear River without difficulty. During their time with Frémont, the two guides had learned of a trace that ran west from the Bear and threaded its way through four mountain ranges before connecting with the main trail to California. For those going to the goldfields, speed was paramount to all other considerations. Hudspeth and Myers knew that if they could follow the old trace and find water and grass for their animals, they would gain time on parties that had started ahead of them.

On Thursday, July 19, they turned off the primary trail and rolled west toward the Portneuf Range, where they discovered a hot springs, which later travelers dubbed "Dempsey's Bath Tub" (today, Lava Hot Springs). From there, they wound through the Bannock Range, crossed the Arbon Valley and dipped below the Deep Creek Mountains to Twin Springs. Their route picked its way over the Sublett Range, then pushed almost due west to the Raft River and the California Trail, a bit beyond.

To Ben Hudspeth's chagrin, when the wagon train connected with the California Trail, he was only eighty miles from Fort Hall. His bypass had trimmed just twenty-five miles off the regular track, saving only two days' travel.

Hudspeth and Myers took one more detour before reaching California, following the route Peter Lassen had blazed a year earlier. Unlike Hudspeth's Cutoff, the Lassen Cutoff proved to be longer and more arduous than the normal line.

The Hudspeth brothers arrived in Sacramento the end of September, sold their cargo for a handsome profit, and soon filed on gold claims in the Sierra Nevada foothills. Some stories say that Ben Hudspeth won a small fortune, racing the thoroughbred his father had given him. If he did, he never lived to enjoy it. On November 16, 1850, Ben Hudspeth died from natural causes near Sutter's Fort.

Ben Hudspeth's legacy was the 130-mile shortcut he

and John Myers had pioneered across eastern Idaho. Their dust had hardly settled before other "Forty-niners" began bypassing Fort Hall. Within a few years, even Oregon-bound emigrants opted to save a couple of miles by skirting the old Hudson's Bay trading post. With its customers siphoned away by Hudspeth's Cutoff, Fort Hall was abandoned in 1856.

* * * * *

LAVA HOT SPRINGS: From Pocatello drive south 20 miles on I-15, taking Exit 47 at McCammon. Lava Hot Springs is 12 miles east on US 30.

Ten-meter diving tower at the "world famous" Lava Hot Springs swimming pool.

Fed daily by over three million gallons of underground water, this "world famous" Olympic-size swimming and mineral pool complex is owned and operated by
the State of Idaho. Visitors may soak in 104° to 112° mus-
cle-soothing comfort at the mineral baths or frolic in the
one-third acre AAU world class swimming pool. The ten-
meter diving tower will challenge even the most venture-
some daredevil. For those who misjudge their dives,
massage therapy is available at the State Foundation baths.
Mailing address: Lava Hot Springs Foundation, P. O. Box
669, Lava Hot Springs, ID 83246.

SHEEP ROCK (today known as Soda Point): To see the
starting point of Hudspeth's Cutoff, drive 17 miles east
from Lava Hot Springs on US 30. Sheep Rock (Soda Point)
is visible in the elbow of the Bear River on the south side
of the highway (1 mile east from the junction of State
Highway 34 and 5 miles west of Soda Springs).

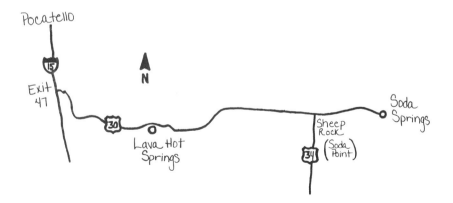

19

Chief Pocatello

Mention "Pocatello," and most people immediately form a mental image of Idaho's second largest city. In the early 1860s, however, "Pocatello" elicited a far different response.

To the Mormon farmers in Cache Valley and the emigrant pioneers trudging along the California Trail or Hudspeth's Cutoff, the name "Pocatello" raised the hair on the backs of their necks. Even its whisper caused grown men to glance nervously over their shoulders, half-expecting to see the Shoshone chief riding hell-bent-for-leather at the head of a shrieking war party. Parents used him like a bogeyman to frighten their children into obedience, warning them that they had better be good or Pocatello would steal them away.

Yet in contrast, the Northwestern Shoshones said "Pocatello" with pride. Hearing their chief's name, the tribe's teenage warriors always stood a bit straighter, hopeful that if Pocatello was nearby, he would take notice and invite them on his next raid. Like their elders, the young men prayed that their respected leader would find a way to reverse the tide of white migration.

Pocatello was born around 1815 in Grouse Creek Valley, west of the Great Salt Lake. In those years, the Northwestern Shoshones to whom he belonged ranged from the present-day Nevada-Utah border to Bear Lake and from the Salt Lake Valley to the Snake River.

Pocatello called himself "Tonaioza," meaning Buffalo Robe. Historians differ on how he obtained the name "Pocatello," although some speculate that it was given to him by the whites, who spelled it every way from "Koctallo" to "Pocataro."

He came of age during the mountain man era, when huge trapping brigades from the Hudson's Bay, American and Rocky Mountain fur companies crisscrossed his homeland, decimating the beaver. Although there is no record of it, he might have gone with his father to the second trapper rendezvous, held in lower Cache Valley in 1826, or to the gathering the following year at the south end of Bear Lake. Many Shoshones attended these raucous celebrations.

With the invasion of the fur brigades, the Northwestern Shoshones began acquiring horses. By the time Pocatello reached his mid-twenties, the tribe's evolution to a horse culture was complete. Hunting parties now roamed far afield, searching for buffalo. As the 1830s drew to a close, trading posts such as forts Hall and Boise displaced the rendezvous supply system in providing the muskets, gunpowder and lead on which the Indians had become dependent.

During the 1840s, Pocatello's standing within his band grew. His people sought his advice about everything from where to move the village to when the salmon runs would start on the Snake River.

While Pocatello's reputation gradually spread among all the Northwestern Shoshones, the trickle of white migration that had begun with fifty-eight people in 1841 swelled to a tidal wave. The discovery of gold at Sutter's Mill drew 25,000 Forty-niners to the California Trail in 1849 and another 44,000 in 1850. The floodgates were open. Each day during the late summer, hundreds of wagons and thousands of cattle lumbered and plodded across the southeastern Idaho countryside.

Meantime, in the southern reaches of the Shoshones' homeland, Brigham Young found the isolation for which he had been searching. By the mid-1850s, over 30,000 Latter Day Saints had settled in the valleys east of the Great Salt Lake. Each year, the Mormon farms crept northward, further encroaching on the Shoshones' territory.

Pocatello and his people watched with alarm as the emigrant hordes frightened away the game and the Mormons' cattle destroyed the grass on which the Shoshones grazed their horses. Faced with starvation, Pocatello and his warriors began to confront the wagon trains and Mormon homesteads, demanding tribute.

Adopting the logic that it was "better to feed 'em than fight 'em," Brigham Young encouraged the Mormons to give the Indians food. In contrast, the overland emigrants usually refused to share their stores, preferring to keep the Indians at bay with rifles and lead. Every year the Shoshones became increasingly combative as the white influx usurped more and more of their country.

By August, 1858, when the Second US Cavalry established Camp Floyd (to monitor the Mormons) in Cedar Valley, west of Utah Lake, Pocatello's renown as a war chief had led the whites to blame him for every Indian skirmish between Bear Lake and the Raft River. The next year when members of a wagon train murdered two Indians on Hudspeth's Cutoff, a twenty-man war party retaliated by killing six emigrants and wounding seven others. During a parley with Pocatello sometime after the fight, Lieutenant Ebenezer Gay clapped him in irons. Although

Gay's commander later released the chief after determining that he hadn't been on the raid, Pocatello learned firsthand the one-sided nature of the white man's justice.

In 1861, the rumor that Pocatello had wiped out a wagon train near the City of Rocks raced through the settlements like wildfire. Newspapers railed; hotheads demanded his scalp; politicians begged for army protection. Every white man and woman in the territory rushed to believe that the Shoshone chief had massacred nearly 300 people. Yet the entire story was a lie. There had been no attack.

Beginning with the town of Franklin, the settlements spread north from Utah into Idaho. Contemptuously dismissing the Shoshones' ancestral claims, the homesteaders robbed the Indians of their land and ripped it apart with plows. Eager to supply the mining camps that were springing up in the Boise Mountains of Idaho and in the rugged terrain of western Montana, merchants and farmers forged new trails like the Salt Lake Road between Brigham City, Utah, and the City of Rocks, and the Montana Trail between Franklin and the Helena goldfields. Pack mules and freight caravans now added to the traffic trespassing over the Shoshones' land.

Desperate to drive the whites from his country, in August, 1862, Pocatello lashed out at wagon trains near the City of Rocks. A few days later, his warriors struck two small emigrant parties on the south side of the Snake River. Here, a bit downstream from the American Falls (now the site of Idaho's Massacre Rocks State Park), the Shoshones killed five white men before making off with several horses. The next day, three dozen men from the two trains set out in pursuit. The Indians soon routed the fledgling posse, killing four of its members. The death of a young girl who was wounded in the initial assault brought the total of white dead to ten.

City of Rocks National Reserve, a favorite campsite for the
thousands of emigrants who traveled the California Trail.

Throughout the autumn of 1862, the unrest continued to boil. Meanwhile, with the nation's attention turned
toward the Civil War, the US Army ordered Colonel
Patrick Connor and the Third California Infantry to Utah
in order to relieve the regular troops, who had gone east to
fight the Confederates. In October, Connor and his
"California Volunteers" established Camp Douglas on a
high bench overlooking Salt Lake City. Their orders were
to guard the Overland Mail, keep an eye on the Mormons
and stop Indian hostility. Frustrated that he wasn't
allowed to join the "real war" against the South, Connor
opted to pacify the Shoshones.

That winter, while the Volunteers marched through
the snow toward Idaho, Pocatello and his band visited
another village of Shoshones, led by Chief Bear Hunter,
which was camped near the Bear River about twelve miles
north of Franklin. On January 28, 1863, Pocatello and his
group bid their friends good-bye and rode away.

At dawn the next day, Connor's militia swept over
Chief Bear Hunter's Shoshones like a whirlwind. The ensu-
ing bloodbath—men, women and children—was the
worst slaughter of Native Americans in the history of the
United States.

The following May, Connor again headed north,
seeking to capture or kill the Shoshones who had escaped
him on the Bear River, particularly Pocatello. From the
camp Connor established near Soda Springs, the Colonel
sent out patrols, but they didn't find the elusive chief
who, with his band, had slipped east to the Green River.

The defeat of Bear Hunter broke the Shoshones' will
to fight. In early July, Chief Washakie negotiated a peace
treaty on behalf of the Eastern Shoshones. Then two
weeks later, Pocatello sent word that he too wished a
truce.

On July 30, 1863, Pocatello and eight other

Northwestern Shoshone chiefs signed the Treaty of Box Elder (Utah) with Connor and Indian Superintendent James Doty. In exchange for peace, Pocatello's people forfeited over two-thirds of their land. Henceforth, they would be restricted to the country lying between the Raft River and Portneuf Mountains. Further, the Indians agreed to permit free passage through their territory by wagon trains, telegraph crews, stagecoaches and the railroad. In return, the government promised the Shoshones a meager $5,000 per year in food and blankets.

Over the next three months, Superintendent Doty secured similar treaties with the Western Shoshones, Gosiutes and several small hybrid bands living near the Bear River.

From the start, the annuities were never sufficient to care for all the Indians. That the supplies were invariably late and always short merely made a bad situation intolerable. Rather than see his people starve, Pocatello began looting food from the stagecoach relay stations that Ben Holladay was stringing across northern Utah and southeastern Idaho. When Holladay complained to the Army, Patrick Connor—now a general—threw Pocatello in jail, vowing to rid himself of the troublesome chief, once and for all. However, after the Superintendent cautioned Connor that there would be a full-blown Indian war if Pocatello were hanged, the General turned the chief loose.

Over the years, the Mormons had always been far more sympathetic to the Shoshones' plight than had either the Army or non-Mormons. After the tribal elders signed the peace treaties, the inadequate government rations compelled their people to beg at Mormon farms. When the Saints gave the Indians food, gentile settlers in southeastern Idaho and northern Utah viewed the kindness with suspicion, fearing that the Mormons might induce the Shoshones to pillage the non-Mormon homesteads. Gentile newspapers further inflamed the racial and religious prejudice of their readers by printing false stories about Indian atrocities.

When the Fort Hall Reservation opened in the late 1860s, Indian agents pressed the Shoshones and Bannocks to give up their traditional homeland and settle there. During the next several years, the scattered Indian bands, including Pocatello's, drifted onto the reservation, lured by the government's promise of increased rations. Of course, the annuities weren't sufficient to feed all the people that the soldiers crowded onto the reservation, so the Indians continued begging at Mormon farms.

Eager for the larger handouts that came to those who embraced the LDS religion, Pocatello went to Salt Lake City in May, 1875, where he was baptized and ordained a church elder.

During this time, the government moved Shoshones from Wyoming's Wind River Mountains and Idaho's Lemhi country onto the Fort Hall Reservation, further stretching the meager annuities. Driven by hunger, other Indians followed in Pocatello's footsteps and headed to Utah to be baptized; by the end of July, the number of Native American proselytes approached 600.

Alarmed by this growing exodus to the Mormon enclaves, northern Utah gentiles petitioned the Army at Camp Douglas to force the Indians back on the reservation. The post commander warned the Shoshones that he would send out the cavalry unless they returned to Idaho. Believing him, Pocatello and the other converts fled to Fort Hall.

Now in his sixties, Pocatello kept to the country near Bannock Creek, avoiding the agency headquarters and the political wrangling that occupied the other chiefs. During the Bannock War of 1878, he stayed on the reservation and didn't fight. His last official appearance occurred on

November 14, 1881, when he added his name alongside the other tribal leaders, agreeing to sell part of the Fort Hall Reservation.

Over the following three years, Pocatello's health deteriorated. By October, 1884, he knew the end was at hand. At his behest, his family and friends took him to the Snake River, above the American Falls. He died a few days later. As he had requested, his wives tied his guns, knives and other possessions to his body, and several of the young men buried him in a large, aquifer-fed spring. In tribute to his memory, the Indians then killed eighteen of Pocatello's ponies and sank them on top of him.

Today, Pocatello's grave lies beneath the American Falls Reservoir.

* * * * *

Pioneer inscriptions written in axle grease at the City of Rocks National Reserve.

CITY OF ROCKS NATIONAL RESERVE: From I-84 Exit 216 (between Burley and the I-84/I-86 interchange) drive south on State Highway 77 approximately 31 miles, turning west (right) on the Elba-Almo Road for another 17 miles. From the National Park Service office in Almo, continue south 0.7 miles and turn west (right) on the City of Rocks Road. The Reserve entrance is 1.6 miles ahead. Primitive camping is available. Mailing address: City of Rocks National Reserve, P. O. Box 169, Almo, ID 83312-0169.

The first known white men to see the City of Rocks were members of a Hudson's Bay Company fur trapping

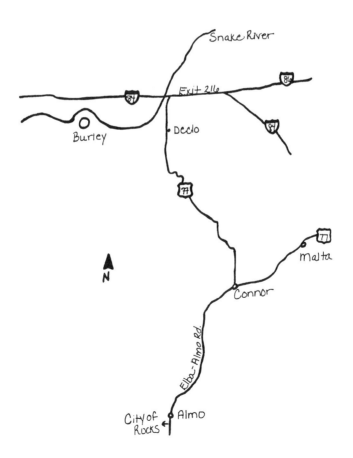

brigade, led by Peter Skene Ogden in 1826. With the start of the California gold rush in 1849, the number of annual visitors to the area jumped precipitously, with 52,000 emigrants camping there in 1852 alone.

Many travelers on the California Trail wrote their names with axle grease on the Reserve's granite boulders. Some of the signatures are still visible.

Today, the City of Rocks is one of the premier rock climbing areas in the United States, offering hundreds of technical climbing routes on monoliths such as the Bread Loaves, Bath Rock and the Dolphin. "Hard men" and beginners alike can find ample challenge.

For those who prefer keeping their feet on the ground, the City has numerous hiking trails. Each spring and early summer, wildflowers transform the meadows into colorful mosaics, while in the fall, yellow- and red-leafed aspens paint the hillsides with fiery hues.

The Reserve is home to deer, elk, coyotes and porcupines. Birds include golden eagles, hawks, doves and vultures. There are also rattlesnakes.

Whether your interest lies in history, rock climbing, hiking, or merely visiting beautiful places, the City of Rocks has something for you.

20

THE MULLAN TREE

On July 4, 1861, a young Army officer stood in the dense forest of Idaho's panhandle, watching one of his soldiers brand the date and the initials "M.R." into a tall pine tree. During the past two years, Captain John Mullan had seen "M.R." emblazoned 624 times, once for every mile of his Mullan Road.

Of course, the War Department never intended that the road be named for its builder. The initials meant "Military Road." But in truth, even though the Army was paying its $230,000-cost, the road belonged to John Mullan.

The need for such a road had existed since 1848, when the US Congress established the Oregon Territory, a vast land that included the present states of Oregon, Washington and Idaho, plus big pieces of western Wyoming and Montana.

On the Missouri River, steamboats could go as far as Fort Benton, Montana; while on the Columbia, shallow-draft vessels could reach the old fur trading post where Wallula, Washington currently sits. Yet in between these ports stood an impenetrable barrier: the Bitterroot Mountains.

In 1854 when Mullan was two years out of West Point, he rode over 1,000 miles as he crisscrossed the northern Continental Divide six times, seeking a suitable passage. After receiving his recommendation, the Army filed it away.

By 1858 population growth in the Pacific Northwest had fueled Indian unrest, compelling a link between the region's two principal waterways. The Army resurrected Mullan's dusty report, secured a Congressional appropriation, and ordered Mullan to begin construction.

Because a road already existed from the river port at Wallula to Fort Walla Walla, Mullan's brigade of 100

Original Mullan Road in the Fourth of July Canyon.

enlisted men, three officers and 100 civilians started working from the Army post in late June the following year.
Within a month, they reached the wetlands at the south
end of Coeur d'Alene Lake.

Further progress required that Mullan's crews build
a 60-foot bridge over the marshes, establish a ferry across
the St. Joe River, and lay endless yards of log corduroy. On
August 18, 1859, at the Cataldo Mission (Idaho's oldest
standing building), the mileage marker read "M.R. 199
Miles."

Alarmed about having a "white man's" road on their
land, the Coeur d'Alene Indians began to foment trouble.
Determined that nothing would halt his progress, Mullan
warned the chiefs that he would hang any who interfered.
None did.

Pushing east from the mission, the workmen hacked
through the mountainous terrain alongside the Coeur
d'Alene River. For days on end, Mullan's road grew not by
the mile but by the foot, each earned with muscle and
sweat.

Using axes and saws, the crews attacked trees that
grew as thick as grass. Where the hillsides steepened and
the streams frothed white, the men dug their trail into the
slopes and built so many bridges that history has lost
count. Wielding an indomitable will, Mullan kept his men
at their task, even squelching a rumor of gold when one of
them found color.

Winter forced everyone into camp. Mullan chafed at
the inactivity, but at least his road had reached the eastern
slope of the Bitterroots. He was now in Montana.

In February, 1860, crews jumped ahead to the Clark
Fork River, built a ferry, then headed up its right bank. It
was late March before other crews could continue chop-
ping and shoveling their way down from the mountains.
The link-up took until the end of June.

Using the valley carved by the Clark Fork, Mullan ran his road seventy miles past the future Missoula town site, then swung east toward the Continental Divide, which he crested on July 17. Beyond this mountainous rib, the gently rolling plains of the upper Missouri River offered easier passage. On August 1, 1860, a day after his thirtieth birthday, Mullan watched the 624-mile marker set at Fort Benton.

The Mullan Road, as it was nicknamed, slashed a twenty-five-foot-wide swath through 120 miles of dense timber, most of them in Idaho. If placed end to end, its road cuts would extend over thirty miles. And every river and stream was spanned with a bridge or ferry.

Promoted to captain, Mullan spent the next two years repairing and altering his original route. In 1861 he relocated the road around the north end of Coeur d'Alene Lake, then drove east to tie into the original Mullan Road

Memorial to John Mullan in the Fourth of July Canyon.

at the Cataldo Mission. On Independence Day that year, his crews were hard at work in the Coeur d'Alene Mountains when one of his men branded the date into what is now call the Mullan Tree.

John Mullan's road never received the traffic he had envisioned. By the time he died in 1909, the forest had reclaimed most of his labor. But history has proven the wisdom of his route. Today in Idaho and western Montana, Interstate 90 follows much of the Mullan Road.

* * * * *

MULLAN TREE HISTORICAL SITE: Take Exit 28 off I-90 in the Fourth of July Canyon, 13 miles east of Coeur d'Alene. From the state historical sign, follow the paved road downhill toward a statue of John Mullan. A one-half-mile walking trail leads past the tree's stone monument; part of the trail follows a remnant of the Mullan Road.

In 1962 a windstorm broke the top off the Mullan Tree. In 1988 its blazed stump was removed to the Museum of North Idaho, where it's on display. The museum is located at 115 N W Boulevard, Coeur d'Alene, ID 83816.

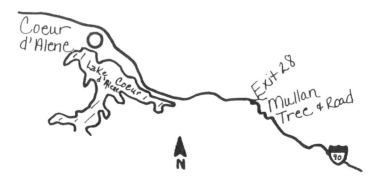

21

The Bear River Massacre

The young soldiers in Colonel Patrick Connor's California Volunteers shivered in their saddles as dawn slowly erased the shadows off the Bear River's icy banks. To the north, smoke from the clustered tepees heralded that the Shoshones hadn't run. Even the greenest blue-clad recruit knew the Indians would fight.

Across the river from the troopers, a lone brave reined in his steaming pony. For the past quarter hour the warrior had raced to and fro, taunting the soldiers to attack. Now, as his mount pawed the frozen ground for a tuft of grass, the Shoshone sat in silence. Among the Volunteers, the crisp air amplified the sounds of waiting: the squeak of leather, sloshing canteens, the neighs of nervous horses, muffled coughs.

"Major McGarry!"

"Sir?"

"Move 'em out!"

At the Colonel's command, the soldiers plunged their horses into the frigid stream. The animals balked at the cold until the cavalrymen raked their flanks with spurs.

After coming out of the water, the Major formed his troop into fours-abreast. A moment later, the bugler signaled "charge," propelling the rank toward a ravine where Chief Bear Hunter and his warriors lay hidden.

Before leaving California, Colonel Connor had petitioned Army headquarters, asking to take his soldiers east to fight the Confederates. Instead of granting the request, the brass sent Connor to Utah to keep an eye on the Mormons. In October, 1862, the disgruntled commander erected Camp Douglas near the Latter Day Saint enclaves east of the Great Salt Lake.

When some Shoshones killed a white miner outside of Franklin, in present-day Idaho, Connor opted to vent his ire on Indians instead of southern rebels. It didn't matter to Connor that the Shoshones had probably shot the

Bear River Crossing on a bleak January day, looking much like it did over a century ago when Patrick Connor's California Volunteers launched the bloodiest Indian massacre in the history of the United States.

man out of desperation. Every year they watched increasing numbers of whites invade eastern Idaho, driving the Indians from their homeland, ripping the earth with plows, wasting the game, and slaughtering Indian ponies. None of this made any difference to the Colonel as he marched his troops up Cache Valley in the sub-zero temperatures, reaching the Bear River village in late afternoon, January 28, 1863.

Just after sunrise the next morning, Connor launched the bloodiest Indian massacre in the history of the United States.

Bear Hunter's warriors met the cavalry charge with a withering barrage of arrows and lead. Fourteen soldiers tumbled dead on the snowy plain before Major McGarry ordered his troopers to fight on foot.

As soon as the infantry forded the river and joined the cavalry's line, Colonel Connor sent part of his force to flank the Indian stronghold. Within minutes the Shoshones were caught in a lethal cross fire. Outgunned, those still alive bolted for their village, hoping to save their families.

With "Take no prisoners!" echoing in their ears, the California Volunteers descended on the fleeing tribe. When the soldiers finished their wanton butchery, the white ground coursed red with blood. The hacked and punctured bodies of Indian men, women and children littered the snow-draped landscape as though they were human cordwood scattered by a vengeful whirlwind.

Counting those who later died from their wounds, Colonel Connor lost twenty-two men, most in the initial assault. The families of Franklin cared for the injured soldiers until they could return to Camp Douglas. But before reaching the warmth of the Mormon homes, seventy-nine troopers saw their fingers and toes blackened by frostbite.

The Shoshones mourned 368 dead, including Chief

Bear Hunter. Barely a handful of warriors escaped. Among
the women and children, the soldiers spared only 164.

Over two and one-half times more Indians were
killed in this southeastern Idaho battle than fell at either
Sand Creek or Wounded Knee.

In the aftermath of the carnage, the Army pinned a
"victory" star to Patrick Connor's collar, promoting him to
Brigadier General. The Shoshones received a far more
dubious reward. Disheartened by the defeat, the surviving bands made peace with the US Government. Then in a
series of treaties, a broken people was forced to sign away
its tribal birthright.

* * * * *

BEAR RIVER MASSACRE MONUMENT: Located on US 91,
3 miles north of Preston and 31 miles south of I-15 Exit 36;
the turnout is 0.5 miles north of the Bear River bridge. The
concrete monument was erected by the Daughters of Utah
Pioneers and is now a National Historic Landmark.

Much of the actual battle site is on private land; to
see it, drive 50 yards north of the memorial, turning west
on Hot Springs Road; in 0.1
mile go right on 1500 W;
after 0.2 miles cross an irrigation ditch and park at the
gate. Most of the slaughter
took place below, in Battle
Creek Ravine (unfortunately,
now used as a dump). The
massacre site can also be
seen from the west side of US
91 just as it starts up the
grade about 0.2 miles north
of the monument.

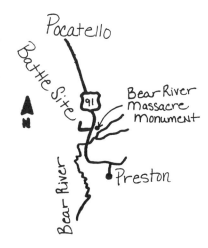

22

WHEN THE CAMELS
RETURNED TO IDAHO

In 1866, in the mountainous mining country a bit west of Helena, Montana, a greenhorn hunter named Tom McNear spotted a half dozen camels in a small clearing. McNear had recently left his native Iowa and had never seen a camel. Thinking they were moose, he sighted his rifle on the nearest one and fired.

"Arrêtez! Arrêtez! Are you crazy?" A man, who McNear hadn't seen, dashed forward frantically waving his arms and screaming with a heavy French accent.

"Get down 'fore you scare 'em off," McNear responded in a stern whisper.

"I think your head, she's cracked," replied the Frenchman. "Why you shoot my camels?"

"Camels? I thought they were moose!"

Tom McNear's error cost him $300 and a red face every time he entered a saloon and someone felt compelled to relate how McNear had obtained his unusual nickname: "Camel."

In the 1860s, camel caravans traversed Idaho, carrying supplies to the gold mines in western Montana. From the settlements in the Washington Territory, these pack trains followed the Mullan Road across Idaho's panhandle, and from the Mormon enclaves of the Utah Territory, they used the Montana-Salt Lake Trail, which led from Cache Valley, past Eagle Rock (now Idaho Falls), and over the Continental Divide at Monida Pass. The Frenchman's camels had just made one of these treks when the hapless McNear mistook them for moose.

The idea to use camels as pack animals had come from Jefferson Davis when he was Secretary of War. In the late 1850s, Davis imported seventy-four North African and Arabian dromedaries to supply the Army's western garrisons. In theory it seemed a good idea, since camels could haul stores over grades that would break wagon teams of horses or mules. But like other theories that look good on paper, this one had its problems.

When confronting a camel on the trail, horses and mules recoiled as though they'd come face-to-face with a grizzly. Should a packer prod a camel too forcefully, he would likely end up combing a handful of pungent, green cud out of his beard. When they spit, camels have uncanny aim.

Eventually, the Army tired of Jefferson Davis's experiment and sold the camels to independent packers, who planned on using them to supply the west's remote mines. Although the new owners did learn to tolerate the camels' touchy temperaments and their capacity to strike terror in more traditional pack stock, they never devised a means to protect the dromedaries' tender feet. Bred for desert sand, the camels quickly went lame when walking over rocky trails. Every trip required that they be allowed to rest and mend, which is what the Frenchman's herd was doing when Tom McNear shot one.

In the early 1870s, the packers abandoned their dromedaries, returning to the more efficient mule trains and wagons. Idaho's camels disappeared—for a second time. Beginning with the Miocene, nearly twenty-four million years ago, prehistoric camels thrived in a southern Idaho that was far more humid and lush than it is today. The animals lasted through the Pliocene Epoch as the state slowly became more arid. However, the ice ages of the Pleistocene led to their demise; they vanished along with the woodland musk-ox and mastodon.

In 1959-60, Ruth Gruhn, a graduate student from Radcliffe College, unearthed evidence of Idaho's prehistoric camel. During her dig at Wilson Butte Cave, northwest of Eden, the young archaeologist determined that camels were hunted by man as recently as 10,500 years ago.

* * * * *

Wilson Butte Cave on the Snake River Plain, where prehistoric man once hunted camels.

WILSON BUTTE CAVE: Leave I-84 at Twin Falls Exit 173, heading north on US 93. In 5.6 miles, turn east on State Highway 25; in 9.2 miles, at the state historical sign about the Minidoka Japanese Relocation Center, turn left on Hunt Road. In 4.3 miles, turn left on Eden Road, which eventually changes from asphalt to dirt. Do not drive when wet! In 5.4 miles, cross the North Side Canal; the piles of lava lining the banks are from its excavation. Bear right beyond the cattle guard and continue another 2.6 miles. Swing left for 200 yards toward the prominent rocky mound, Wilson Butte Cave.

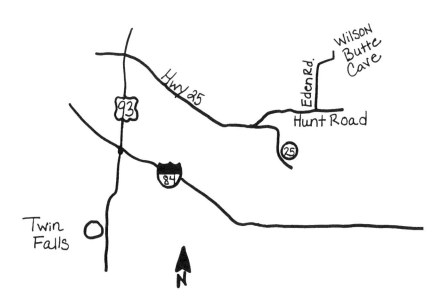

23

IDAHO'S CAMAS WAR

The Treaty of 1868 assigned Idaho's Bannocks to the Fort Hall Indian Reservation, a swath of land along the Portneuf River, at that time about the size of Delaware and Rhode Island combined. The treaty also granted the Bannocks unrestricted access to the Camas Prairie, near present-day Fairfield.

Every spring, blue camas lilies carpeted this lush plain with flowers. For countless generations, the Bannocks had harvested the onion-shaped camas bulbs when they matured in late summer. However, during the bureaucratic meandering that led to the treaty's ratification, "Camas Prairie" somehow became "Kansas Prairie," a place that didn't exist. Still, the tribal elders were unconcerned. Their grandmothers' grandmothers had dug the nutritious bulbs, and the US Government had given its word. The Camas Prairie belonged to the Bannocks, and they thought it always would.

In the 1870s, the Army resettled Shoshones from Wyoming onto the Fort Hall Reservation, compelling them to compete with the Bannocks for government rations. Federal bungling and indifference, compounded by graft,

Idaho's Camas Prairie beneath the Soldier Mountains.
Today green patchwork farms color the landscape
where camas lilies once painted it in violet and blue.

ensured that the allotments were always short. As Indian
fathers watched their families go hungry, their resentment
grew. Each year their unrest was fueled by the white farmers and miners who crowded into southeastern Idaho,
overrunning the hunting grounds, wasting the deer and
elk, killing the Indians' ponies for "sport," and tearing
apart the earth with steel plows.

In 1877, Chief Buffalo Horn offered his Bannock
scouts to General Howard in order to chase down the fleeing Nez Perce. When forty Army horses were stolen,
Howard blamed the Bannocks, jailing several. Although
Buffalo Horn proclaimed his scouts' innocence, Howard
refused to free the prisoners until the animals were
returned.

Buffalo Horn quit the Army in disgust, retiring to the Fort Hall Reservation. Throughout that autumn and winter, the chief railed against the white man's injustice. He was especially contemptuous of the Army, citing Custer's defeat by the Sioux in 1876 and General Howard's humiliating campaign against the Nez Perce as examples of how inept the troopers were in battle. To the angry warriors who listened, Buffalo Horn's call for revenge struck a chord.

In May, 1878, settlers, taking advantage of the "Kansas Prairie" clerical error, herded hogs onto the Bannocks' Camas Prairie. The hogs quickly uprooted and ate the succulent bulbs. A week or so later when Buffalo Horn and some of the tribe visited the prairie, they were appalled at the destruction. After Bill Silvey, Lew Kensler and George Nesbit drove a large herd of cattle and horses onto the plain, Indian tempers reached a boil.

On May 28, two Bannocks rode into Silvey's camp as the stockmen were finishing breakfast. Whether or not the warriors planned to fight or were provoked is lost to history, but one of the Indians drew his revolver and shot Nesbit in the mouth, severing his tongue. As Kensler lunged for his rifle, a bullet grazed his scalp. At a spring a few yards away, Silvey dove for cover as more shots dusted the dirt near his feet. Ignoring his bleeding head, Kensler fired his Winchester as the Bannocks sprinted for their horses. He thought he wounded one, but he wasn't sure.

Needing a doctor for Nesbit, the stockmen rode to another cow camp about sixteen miles away. From there, other gallopers soon raced to inform the Army at Fort Boise.

Meanwhile, a dozen or more Bannocks plundered the Silvey camp, driving off fifteen horses. Around a council fire that night, Buffalo Horn persuaded 200 of the tribe to follow him on the warpath. Southern Idaho ignited like dry tinder.

At Glenns Ferry, the Indians crossed the Snake River, then cut the boat lines. A few miles later, they came on some freight wagons that were returning from Nevada. The Bannocks killed the three teamsters, then looted the wagons, which contained several jugs of whiskey. While the war party celebrated its victory, a Bannock named Bruneau John decided he'd had enough fighting. Leaving his companions to consume the liquor, he rode to Bruneau Valley and warned the settlers to flee. When Buffalo Horn's warriors finally reached the area, they found nothing but empty homesteads.

On May 31, telegrams alerted General Howard's headquarters in Portland, Oregon. By early June, Army posts throughout the territory were dispatching soldiers to quell what everyone feared would be a general uprising. From Fort Boise, Captain Reuben Bernard led a cavalry troop after Buffalo Horn, while Idaho's most famous lawman, Orlando "Rube" Robbins, brought along thirty-five volunteer scouts.

After learning that the Bannocks were raiding the nearby countryside, twenty-six miners from Silver City in Owyhee County confronted Buffalo Horn and sixty warriors near South Mountain. The miners attacked on horseback, but the well-hidden Indians held their ground. Outgunned, the white militia attempted to withdraw, prompting the chief to counterattack. Just when it appeared that Buffalo Horn would win a great victory, an "unlucky" shot killed him. Distracted by their leader's death, the Bannocks allowed the miners to escape. The chastened militia scurried home to Silver City in time to see Captain Bernard arrive with his soldiers.

On June 12, General Howard reached Fort Boise, determined to prevent another humiliation similar to the one he'd suffered at the hands of the Nez Perce. Soon, tele-graph wires across the entire region hummed with urgent messages summoning troops.

After the Battle of South Mountain, the Bannocks headed to eastern Oregon, where other tribes joined the campaign to recapture their lost homeland. A Paiute war chief named Egan now became the nominal leader. Meanwhile, Captain Bernard's command left Silver City and trailed after the hostiles; some days the troopers cov-ered fifty miles. Near the end of June, the Captain located the Indians' camp, which according to Army estimates was bustling with 2,000 men, women, and children. That night, the handful of scouts under Rube Robbins launched a furious sneak attack against the sleeping tribes. Panicked, the Indians fled directly into Bernard's blocking force of 250 cavalrymen.

During the melee, which continued until after dawn, Chief Egan spotted Robbins. In a confrontation reminis-cent of the days of chivalry, the two raging warriors charged each other with their guns blazing. The Paiute hung off the side of his horse, firing from under its neck, while Robbins sat upright in his saddle. Their duel ended when Robbins shattered Egan's wrist with a bullet.

After both sides withdrew to lick their wounds, the Army counted five dead, the Indians nearly 100. For the next couple of days, Captain Bernard rested his exhausted troops and awaited the arrival of General Howard. The pause allowed the Indians to slip away.

In July, the soldiers fought the Indians to a standoff in the Blue Mountains. Again, the hostiles escaped. Then a few days later, other troops caught them near Pendleton, Oregon, handing them a crushing defeat.

Each surviving band now raced for the security of its own reservation. With four companies of cavalry in pursuit, the Bannocks returned to Idaho, pillaging home-

steads along the way. After reaching Fort Hall, the warriors melded with those who hadn't left. Although the
Army sought no further reprisals, it never again allowed
the Bannocks to dig roots on the Camas Prairie.

Camas (Camassia
quamash) belongs to
the lily family. Ranging
from southern British
Columbia to northern
California and eastward
into northern Utah,
Wyoming, Montana,
and Idaho, it prefers
moist meadows. During
the spring, its star-
shaped flowers paint
entire fields in blue and
violet.

When harvested
in August, camas bulbs
are odorless and resem-
ble tiny white onions.
Indians baked the
bulbs in holes, layering
them from bottom to
top with hot stones,

Blooming camas lily. It's difficult
to imagine that such a delicate
flower could have ignited a
bloody war.

grass and alder leaves, camas bulbs, more grass and alder
leaves, soil, and fire. After three days, the bulbs were
removed and dried. Prepared this way, they could be
stored for three years.

Cooked camas roots are brown, smell like dried fruit,
and taste slightly sweet. For a special treat, Indians
enjoyed eating roasted bulbs dipped in beef or buffalo
marrow. The bulbs were used in soups and baked into

camas bread. Lewis and Clark reported eating a few loaves during their journeys across northern Idaho. By boiling cooked camas in water, then mixing the juice with honey, Indians also made a soothing cough syrup.

[Editor's Note: One variety of Camas is deadly poisonous. Great caution should be taken when harvesting camas.]

* * * * *

CAMAS PRAIRIE CENTENNIAL MARSH (near where the attack on Silvey's camp occurred): For those approaching from the east, drive 9 miles west from Fairfield on US 20; at the sign for the Centennial Marsh turn left on Wolf Lane. The one-lane road out to the observation point lies 8 miles beyond; this narrow track to the center of the marsh is sometimes flooded during the spring runoff. Good gravel roads lead around the marsh, returning to US 20 at Hill City. For those coming from the west, take I-84 Exit 95 near Mountain Home and follow US 20 east; at Hill City ignore the sign for the marsh and continue on US 20 for another 5 miles, turning right on Wolf Lane.

Depending on the year, late May through mid-June

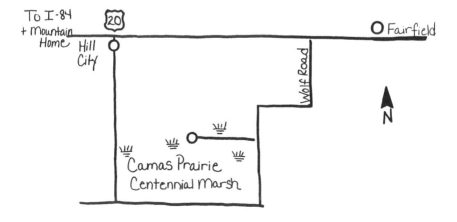

is usually the best time to see the camas in full bloom.
During the nesting season, the marsh is alive with water-
fowl and shorebirds, including mallards, pintails, cinna-
mon teals, shovelers, sandhill cranes, curlews, and avocets,
to name but a few.

24

ORLANDO "RUBE" ROBBINS:
AN IDAHO PALADIN

Deadwood, Tombstone, Dodge City—each of these towns evokes the image of America's frontier, where men such as Wild Bill Hickok, Bat Masterson and the Earp brothers held sway with their six-guns and tin stars. First the dime novels and then Hollywood westerns immortalized these pistoleers, gilding their reputations until fact melded with fantasy.

Idaho, too, had its "Wyatt Earp." Though forgotten by a world that learns its history from the movies, Orlando "Rube" Robbins was every bit as much the bold lawman as were his more famous contemporaries.

Rube Robbins was born in Maine on August 30, 1836. As a teenager, he owned a yoke of oxen, which his father sold without permission. Infuriated, the seventeen-year-old Robbins walked away from his family's farm and headed for the mining camps of California.

At the age of twenty-five, he left California and drifted to the gold strikes in northern Idaho. Then two years later, in August, 1863, he moved to the diggings at Idaho City. The following year he became a deputy sheriff.

The Civil War had polarized the hardened miners of

Orlando "Rube"
Robbins.

*(Courtesy of Idaho Historical
Society #70-1.10)*

Idaho City. Yankee and Rebel sympathizers often settled their differences with their fists or knives. Many a night Robbins had to wade into a drunken melee in order to compel the peace.

Early one summer, a number of southerners boasted that they wouldn't permit any Yankees to sing the Star Spangled Banner on Independence Day. When Robbins heard the bluster, he became incensed. He was a Union man to the core. On July 4, he walked into a saloon filled with southerners. Without saying a word, he hopped atop a billiard table and drew his two revolvers. The raucous crowd immediately fell silent as every eye fixed on his Colts.

"Oh, say can you see by the dawn's early light. . . ?"

Not a person moved as Robbins's voice filled the bar-room with the song's three-quarter time.

". . . O'er the land of the free and the home of the brave?"

After finishing the final note, the young deputy holstered his pistols, climbed down from the table and stepped into the street. No one tried to stop him.

Robbins's repute as a lawman soon carried him to Boise, where he worked as a deputy sheriff and later as a US marshal. During March, 1868, an underground gunfight broke out in Silver City between miners employed by the Golden Chariot and Elmore mines. Known as the Owyhee War, this 100-man battle started when the Golden Chariot's miners tunneled into a shaft belonging to the Elmore.

The subterranean shoot-out lasted three days before Idaho's Territorial Governor sent Robbins to force a truce. The deputy rode from Boise to Silver City in six hours, amazingly fast, considering that the sixty or so miles of roads he covered were no doubt mud-cloaked from the spring rains and snowmelt. Robbins wasted little time bringing the warring factions together. By sundown the day he arrived, he had negotiated an end to the fray.

During Idaho's Indian Wars, Robbins served as head of scouts and a colonel in the territorial militia. The Camas War of the late 1870s found Robbins pursuing Chief Egan and the Bannocks through the Owyhee badlands near South Mountain. At Silver Creek, Robbins and Egan fought perhaps the most bizarre "duel" since the days of Arthurian chivalry.

According to a militia eye witness, Robbins and four of his command were riding over a ridge when they were surprised by a band of Indians. The scouts spurred their horses, trying to get away, while the Bannocks took up the chase. When a scout named Bill Myers was wounded and his horse killed, Robbins turned back, attempting to rescue him.

As Robbins galloped toward Myers, he spotted Chief Egan, who also recognized him. Like two knights errant having been whisked from a medieval time, the Colonel and Chief began jousting with their Winchesters. While their horses circled, these fearless warriors blasted away, oblivious to every other fight except their own.

Their rifles empty, they drew their pistols. Chief Egan's lead tore through Robbins's clothes and nicked his finger. Robbins's bullets also missed their mark as the Chief deftly used his horse's neck for cover. And then a lucky shot hit Egan in the wrist, spilling him off his horse. Stunned, the Chief had barely crawled to his feet when trooper Myers wounded him in the chest.

While Egan's band carried off their fallen leader, Robbins pulled the injured scout up behind his saddle, and they raced toward the Army's lines.

Seven weeks later, Robbins again proved his mettle. He was rowing Lieutenant W. R. Parnell, a bugler and two cavalrymen across the Snake River when a horse they had tied behind their skiff panicked. Just as the men cut the animal loose, it capsized the boat. Parnell and the bugler began swimming, while Robbins boosted one of the cavalrymen atop the overturned hull. The other cavalryman grabbed the horse's tail and was towed to shore.

Seeing the bugler begin to tire, Robbins left the safety of the rowboat and helped him to the shallows. Meanwhile, Lieutenant Parnell started to founder, weighted down by his boots, pistol, and cartridge belt. Robbins again plunged into the current, reaching Parnell as he was about to drown. Robbins kept the officer afloat until another boat came to their aid.

Throughout the 1870s, '80s, and '90s, Robbins

tracked badmen across southern Idaho. In February, 1876, after six bandits robbed the Silver City stagecoach on the outskirts of Boise, the deputy had them behind bars within two days of their crime. In August, 1882, he covered 1,280 miles in thirteen days before catching the outlaw Charley Chambers. The few desperadoes who avoided Robbins's grasp counted themselves fortunate.

Yet, there existed a side to Rube Robbins apart from gunplay and daring. In his thirties, he joined the temperance movement and found religion. After his public baptism in the Boise River, he became president of the Methodist Church Sunday School. He won a term in the Idaho Territorial Legislature, and a few years afterwards, served as its Sergeant at Arms.

In his late sixties, Robbins escorted prisoners to the state penitentiary. Although many of them were one-third his age, none ever escaped.

On May 1, 1908, Idaho's greatest lawman died of a heart attack. After his death, tributes poured forth, each seeking to take his measure. Few came close to the praise uttered years earlier by Cherokee Bob.

As the outlaw lay dying from Robbins's gunshot, he said the marshal never jumped to the side after squeezing the trigger, but "always sprang through the smoke [of his revolver] and advanced upon his opponent, firing as he came."

* * * * *

**Catholic Church at Idaho's most famous ghost town:
Silver City.**

SILVER CITY (the queen of Idaho's ghost towns): Take
the I-84 Business Route into Mountain Home, turning
west on State Highway 67. Near the entrance to the air
base, go right at the sign for Grand View. At State
Highway 78, turn right (northwest) for 25 miles, then left
onto Silver City Road at the state historical markers. Silver
City is 20 miles away. The road is suitable for cars, but
vehicles towing trailers are not advised. It's normally open
from June through October. Start with a full gas tank as no
gas is available in town.

Primitive camping is available in and around Silver
City; take your own water. Rustic, nineteenth-century
accommodations are available at the Idaho Hotel, which
also serves food. Reservations are recommended. Mailing
address: P. O. Box 75, Murphy, ID 83650.

In its prime, Silver City had a population of 2,500. Now summer residents swell the town to 300, but only two or three people live here year-round. On the second weekend of each September, Silver City hosts an open house, offering tours through its historic buildings.

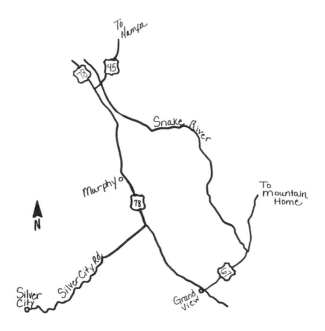

25

Peg Leg Annie of Rocky Bar

During the early 1860s, prospectors began scouring Idaho's Boise Mountains for gold. As they combed the creeks feeding the Feather River, a few of them found the mother lode. Within months, the strike brought miners streaming into the rugged terrain. In their wake flocked gamblers, laundresses, saloon-keepers and merchants. Almost overnight, clapboard cabins sprang up on a gravel bench dubbed "Rocky Bar."

On Independence Day, 1864, Stephen McIntyre came to the fledgling town, seeking his fortune. Beside him walked his wife and son, while perched atop his shoulders rode his four-year-old daughter, Felicia Ann—or Annie, as her family called her.

The ore was rich, and Annie's father prospered, eventually becoming part-owner of the Golden Star Mine.

Rocky Bar also flourished, though its muddy streets seemed as rough as the country. Drunken brawls were commonplace. Arguments over card games, rebel sympathizers wanting to re-fight the Civil War, sometimes just plain orneriness led men to settle their differences with knuckles and guns. The cause is lost to history, but in one

Annie Morrow.

(Courtesy of Idaho Historical Society #81-18.1)

of these mindless melees, Stephen McIntyre was shot dead.

During the 1870s, the surface mines played out, and the fast-money operators left for fresher diggings. All those who didn't move on wondered whether Rocky Bar would wither away like Idaho's other boom-to-bust mining towns.

Annie stayed at the Bar and grew into an attractive young woman, pretty enough to interest Tom Morrow, who married her when she was fourteen. He died several years later, leaving her with a son. (Some reports say she had five children.)

During the 1880s, Annie supported herself with a boarding house and restaurant. Then in mid-decade, English investors revived Rocky Bar, infusing capital to expand mines such as the Elmore. The miners returned, many sleeping under Annie's roof and eating the meals she set on her dining table. Those down on their luck knew they'd never go hungry so long as Annie had the strength to fire up her stove.

Throughout the 1880s and into the '90s, Annie was a fixture of the town. When her coarse language couldn't quell a ruckus, her revolver did. More than once she shot holes in her eatery's ceiling, trying to quiet some drunken loudmouth. Yet despite Annie's lack of gentility, everyone knew her heart held more gold than had ever been panned from Rocky Bar's many streams.

In the spring of 1896, Annie and Emma Soaper (some call her Dutch Em Von Losch) hiked fourteen miles to the sister town of Atlanta. On May 15, they began their journey home in a snowstorm.

Later that day, the mail packer, Will Tate, left Atlanta for Bald Mountain, where he intended exchanging pouches with the mail carrier coming from Rocky Bar. Five miles south of town, Tate caught up with the two women.

Despite the storm, Annie and Emma assured him that they would be fine. Giggling, they told him they had fortified themselves with whiskey and felt quite warm.

After advising them to follow the prints left by his snowshoes, Tate bid them good-bye. By the time he reached the mail packers' cabin near the summit of Bald Mountain, the storm had become a blizzard.

Tate swapped pouches with the Rocky Bar carrier and started his return-trek to Atlanta. His tracks from a few hours before were buried under several inches of snow. Although he didn't see Annie and Emma along the road, he wasn't particularly worried, figuring they must have turned back to wait for fair weather.

After reaching town, Tate inquired about the women, but no one had seen them. He now realized they had to be lost.

The blizzard continued for two more days, forestalling any rescue attempt. The moment the sky cleared, a relief party set out on snowshoes.

When the women were found, Emma was dead, her frozen body wrapped in Annie's undergarments. Snowblind and out of her head, Annie was crawling about on her hands and knees, her feet frostbitten.

The searchers carried Annie to Atlanta, then sent word to Mountain Home for a doctor. Meanwhile, Annie's ankles and feet swelled, turning black and gangrenous. The miners knew she couldn't hold out until the doctor arrived. Unless her legs were amputated, she would die.

The miners gave their feeble friend as much whiskey as she could drink, then tied her down atop a table. Someone suggested they draw straws to see who would perform the operation, but Tug Wilson volunteered. Using a knife and a meat saw, he cut off Annie's legs a few inches above her ankles.

In time, Annie returned to Rocky Bar. After her stumps healed, artificial legs again enabled her to serve meals to her boarders.

Shortly after the turn of the century, she began living with Henry Longheme, who owned a saloon adjacent to her rooming house. In 1924, he took her life savings—$12,000—to deposit in a San Francisco bank. Annie never again saw Longheme or her money.

Soon thereafter, the gold petered out and Rocky Bar's miners drifted away. Peg Leg Annie also moved on and ultimately outlasted the town. When she died in

Mountain Home at the age of seventy-five, Rocky Bar was little more than a fading memory.

The history of Peg Leg Annie has grown into legend. Although there are as many versions of her life as there are story tellers, all speak of her warm heart.

In May 1996, on the 100th anniversary of Annie's amputation, the residents of Atlanta commemorated her ordeal with a "leg roast." Annie was toasted during a delicious dinner that featured leg of lamb.

* * * * *

ROCKY BAR: From I-84 Exit 95 near Mountain Home, drive 26 miles east on US 20, or from Fairfield, drive 25 miles west on US 20. Turn north on the Pine-Featherville

Rocky Bar, where Peg Leg Annie once gave free meals to miners down on their luck.

Road. This paved highway leads 28 miles to Featherville and passes picturesque Anderson Ranch Reservoir. During the summer and early fall, the shoreline is dotted with campers, who come to water-ski and fish. North of the reservoir, the road winds alongside the South Fork of the Boise River, a fly fisherman's dream. Between the reservoir and Featherville are numerous campgrounds and several motel-resorts, which have gas and food. Fifty yards beyond the Featherville Motel, veer left on the unnamed gravel road (Forest Road 156); Rocky Bar is 7 miles away.

As you look at Rocky Bar's few remaining buildings,

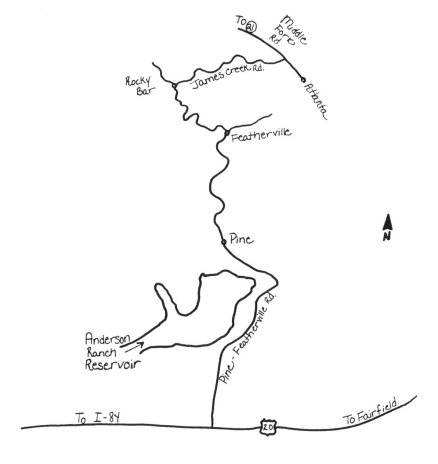

their sideboards weathered by rain and sun, imagine the town as it was in the late 1860s, when it bustled with 2,500 people.

ATLANTA: To reach Atlanta from Rocky Bar, turn right on James Creek Road, which climbs over Bald Mountain, the peak where Annie and Emma became marooned during that fateful spring blizzard in 1896. Although steep and not advised for trailers, the grade is passable for cars. In 13 miles, turn right on Middle Fork Road for another 1 mile.

Atlanta supports a handful of full-time residents and has a store and restaurant/bar. To reach the Middle Fork of the Boise River, go north on Forest Road 205 from the village center. In one mile cross the bridge to a T. The left road follows the river downstream.

26

THE CARLIN DISASTER

"The Clearwater Mountains are an elk hunter's dream," William Carlin told his two friends as they departed Weippe, Idaho, on September 20, 1893. Even their guide, Martin Spencer, as much as guaranteed them trophy-size bulls. With George Colgate, their fifty-two-year-old cook, bringing up the rear, the small hunting party was in high spirits as it rode east into the foothills and picked up the Lolo Trail.

Native Americans had traveled this trace for generations before Lewis and Clark made it famous. In 1866, the Department of Interior sought to turn it into a road, but surveyors deemed the country too rough. Eleven years later, General Howard chased Chief Joseph and 700 Nez Perce over its precipitous contours. The Indians escaped, but the dead horses sacrificed by them and the pursuing troops testified to the route's difficulty.

For the Carlin party, the trail's reputation merely heightened the adventure. When it snowed early in the trip, what should have been a warning was ignored in the excitement of shooting grouse and hooking trout. The men pushed on, forcing their stock over a frozen path

Carlin party.

(Courtesy of Idaho Historical Society #P1997.2.5)

increasingly choked with deadfall. Each mile involved a tiring climb and steep descent.

On September 26, they quit the Lolo Trail and dropped down to the Lochsa River. That afternoon they stumbled upon the half-finished cabin of Jerry Johnson and Ben Keeley, two prospectors who intended spending the winter in the Clearwater wilderness. Johnson warned Carlin that he and his friends ought to get out of the mountains before the passes filled with snow, but the advice went unheeded.

The following morning Colgate begged off his

chores, complaining that it hurt to walk. For years an enlarged prostate had required him to drain his bladder artificially. Embarrassed to perform the procedure before strangers, he had purposely left his catheter at home. Still, he assured everyone that he'd be fine if allowed to rest.

Annoyed but not overly concerned with their cook's health, the hunters spent the next two weeks missing or wounding more elk than they killed. Almost every day it snowed. Meanwhile, uremic poison ballooned Colgate's legs to double their normal size.

At their guide's insistence, the hunters reluctantly agreed to leave on October 10. They headed for the Lolo Trail, but their horses soon floundered in the deep snow. After returning to the Johnson-Keeley cabin, the party faced its plight. Colgate's condition was worsening by the hour. If the cook didn't get to a doctor, he would soon die. He couldn't snowshoe, and the others hadn't the strength to drag him in a sled, especially over such an uncompromising route. Their only hope was the Lochsa River.

Carlin hired Keeley to build two twenty-six-foot rafts and pilot them downstream. The journey began on November 3. In the first hour the raft carrying Colgate broke apart in the rapids. The men fished the cook and their supplies out of the freezing torrent and loaded them on the second boat.

For nine days the party battled channel-clogging boulders and white water, while Colgate deteriorated. Each new mile brought rapids worse than in the one before. Then at Holly Creek the river won. The men discarded their raft. To attempt floating farther meant suicide.

The cook was now so ill he barely knew his own name. Unable to carry him and deeming his condition terminal, the party parceled out its remaining food and continued on foot, leaving Colgate to die.

The steep canyon reduced the pace to a crawl.

Some days the men made little more than a mile; five they considered cause for celebration. Their rations nearly gone, they searched for game but saw little and shot even less. The few trout they caught barely kept them from starving.

Finally on November 22, near the Hellgate Rapids, the exhausted survivors met a rescue party that had been dispatched by Carlin's worried father. Thanksgiving Day found Carlin and his friends enjoying a sumptuous dinner in Kendrick.

No sooner did the newspapers announce that the men were safe than a public outcry attacked them for deserting George Colgate. The paltry twenty-five dollars William Carlin gave Colgate's widow merely fueled the criticism.

The following summer Colgate's bones were located eight miles downstream from where he'd been abandoned, apparently washed there by the spring floods. They were buried near Johnson's cabin at a game lick now dubbed Colgate Warm Springs.

* * * * *

LOCHSA RIVER: This "wild and scenic" river can be approached from Lewiston via US 12 or on State Highway 13 from Grangeville to Kooskia, where the state road intersects US 12. From Kooskia follow US 12 east along the Middle Fork of the Clearwater River; 23 miles later in Lowell, you'll come to the mouth of the Lochsa. From here US 12 parallels the Lochsa for about 70 miles until the river bends south near the Powell Ranger Station. There are numerous Forest Service campgrounds along the highway.

The Lochsa River is a playground for trout fishermen and white water rafters, alike. As you drive past the roaring rapids, imagine trying to run them on a crude log raft as did the Carlin Party.

COLGATE WARM SPRINGS AND GEORGE COLGATE'S GRAVE: Located 61 miles east of Lowell on US 12. The Colgate Licks National Recreation Trail leads north from the parking area to the springs. With luck, you might see elk or deer licking the mineral-laden water. George Colgate's grave is on the east side of the parking area, a bit below the highway.

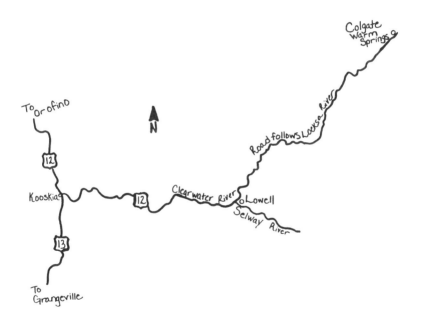

27

THE LEGAL SAGA OF
DIAMONDFIELD JACK

In the mid-1890s, Cassia County stretched west past Salmon Falls Creek to the Owyhee County line. This grassy expanse of south-central Idaho belonged to the cattle ranchers and sheepmen.

A shaky peace existed between the beef and wool barons, its enforcement bolstered by a "deadline" that split Cassia County along the high ground forming its center. The cattle grazed west of this boundary; the sheep ranged east.

When the sheepmen began encroaching in the summer of 1895, the Sparks-Harrell Company, which owned cattle ranches in Idaho and Nevada, hired Jackson Lee Davis as a night rider. His duties were explicit: drive the sheep beyond the deadline.

A miner turned gunman, Davis had acquired his "Diamondfield" nickname because he once prospected for diamonds.

Diamondfield Jack began confronting the sheepmen with his Winchester. Before long, most considered it healthier keeping to their own range. Then in November he wounded a sheepherder who had strayed onto Sparks-

Jack Davis
"Diamondfield Jack."

*(Courtesy of Idaho Historical
Society #77-2.33)*

Harrell land. With the county sheriff in the wool growers' pocket, Davis deemed it safer retreating to Wells, Nevada, until things quieted. His absence soon emboldened the sheepmen to intrude past the deadline.

In late January, 1896, Davis again visited a Sparks-Harrell ranch in southern Idaho. On February 1, he and another night rider, Fred Gleason, shot it out with herders a few miles from the property. Although no one was hit, the incident prompted the gunfighters to hightail it south. They left the ranch at dawn, February 4, pausing for noon dinner at another of the company's ranches just below the state line.

On February 16, two sheepmen were found shot to death on Deep Creek. They'd been murdered the same day Diamondfield Jack and Fred Gleason departed for Nevada. Having few clues other than a corncob pipe and the night riders' reputations, the Albion sheriff issued warrants for the Sparks-Harrell gunmen.

A year passed before Diamondfield Jack came to trial in Albion, the very heart of sheep country. The Idaho Wool Growers Association hired William Borah to assist the prosecutor, while the Sparks-Harrell Company retained James Hawley for the defense.

The prosecution's witnesses said Diamondfield Jack had bragged about shooting sheepherders in Idaho. Whether his drunken boasts pertained to earlier skirmishes or the murders on Deep Creek, a jury of sheepmen was to decide. The defense argued that the accused couldn't possibly have ridden from the Sparks-Harrell ranch to the murder site with enough time to eat noon dinner in Nevada, a distance of fifty-five miles. On April 15, 1897, the jury rendered its verdict: first-degree murder. The judge sentenced Diamondfield Jack to hang.

While Davis awaited execution, the state tried Fred Gleason. After hearing the same evidence that had convicted Diamondfield Jack, the jury found Gleason not guilty.

Defense attorney Hawley then enlisted two cowboys to make the alleged murder-ride. Although they did it in five and one-half hours, both attested it would have taken longer in winter. On this basis, Hawley obtained a stay of execution while he appealed. In June, 1898, the Idaho Supreme Court sustained the original verdict. Diamondfield Jack's hanging was set for October 21.

Eight days before the execution, Jim Bower, a Sparks-Harrell ranch superintendent, and his friend, Jeff Gray, signed affidavits admitting the killings. Bower said the corncob pipe found at the murder scene was his. Despite these confessions, the Idaho Board of Pardons refused to release Diamondfield Jack. Instead, it merely postponed his date with the gallows until December 16, and at the last minute, delayed it again until February 1, 1899.

Hawley now appealed in federal court, which issued another stay. Riders brought the injunction to the Albion jail only hours before Davis was to swing.

A few days later, a new law requiring that all executions take place in the State Penitentiary sent Diamondfield Jack to death row in Boise. Then in December, the Idaho Supreme Court reversed the law, remanding him to Albion.

Meanwhile, the Cassia County District Court ruled that Bower and Gray had acted in self-defense, acquitting them of murdering the same sheepmen Davis had been convicted of killing.

In late 1900, Diamondfield Jack's case reached the US Supreme Court which, because of procedural technicalities, refused to intervene. Hawley then petitioned Cassia County for a new trial, but the district judge denied the request. The trip to the hangman was reset for June 21, 1901.

During this time, many letters begging clemency arrived at the Idaho Board of Pardons, whose members had recently changed. The Board put off the execution two more times while it granted a review, the latter reprieve coming as the Albion townsfolk gathered around the gallows.

On July 16, 1901, the Board added a final irony to this legal farce, commuting Diamondfield Jack's death sentence to life imprisonment. Davis moved back to the state prison in Boise.

Again Hawley appealed to the Idaho Supreme Court, and once more it refused to release his client. Next, the attorney re-solicited the Board of Pardons. The arguments and depositions continued until December 18, 1902, when at long last Diamondfield Jack walked free.

Jack Davis relocated to Tonopah, Nevada, and struck it rich prospecting for gold; however, his newfound wealth soon slipped through his fingers. From 1908 until 1948 little is known of his whereabouts, although he was seen in Mexico, Montana, New York City, and California.

In December, 1948, a Las Vegas taxicab ran over Diamondfield Jack as he stepped off a sidewalk. He died in a Nevada hospital five days later, January 2, 1949.

* * * * *

OLD IDAHO PENITENTIARY: From Boise I-84 Exit 54, take Broadway Avenue north 3 miles; turn right on Warm Springs Avenue for 1 mile, then left on Old Penitentiary Road; mailing address: Old Idaho Penitentiary, 2445 Old Penitentiary Road, Boise, ID 83712.

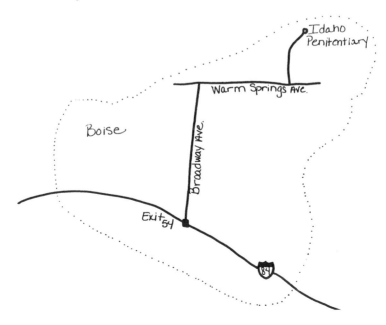

Old Idaho State Penitentiary, where Diamondfield Jack
awaited the hangman's noose.

OLD CASSIA COUNTY COURTHOUSE: From I-84 Exit 216 (9 miles east of Burley and 5 miles west of the I-84/I-86 interchange) drive 12 miles south on State Highway 77 to Albion. The old courthouse is now Arnold's Albion Market at Main and Market streets; the trial was held on the second floor. The Diamondfield Jack historical sign is in the village park alongside the highway.

The ranch from which Diamondfield Jack rode that fateful February morning lies beneath the Salmon Falls Creek Reservoir, just north of Jackpot, Nevada.

28

THE CAREY ACT:
A "MAGIC" LAW

The Homestead Act of 1862 offered land to any man or woman willing to scratch a living from 160 acres of western dirt. The Desert Land Act of 1877 allowed a homesteader in arid regions to settle 640 acres, provided he irrigated his holding within three years.

On the parched plain high above the Snake River, such a task would have taken a millionaire's purse, and millionaires didn't homestead. During the nineteenth century, south-central Idaho belonged to the sagebrush and rattlesnakes.

Then in 1883, Ira Perrine left Indiana, hoping to make a fortune in the silver mines of Idaho's Wood River Valley. After realizing that he could earn more money feeding the miners than digging ore, the lanky young Hoosier acquired a small herd of dairy cattle and began selling milk and butter.

In the autumn of 1884, Perrine drove his herd south for the winter, pasturing it in a grassy nook alongside the Snake River. Over the next decade and a half, this energetic entrepreneur built a thriving farm where today sits the Blue Lakes Country Club of Twin Falls. Watered by spring-fed pools, the fertile volcanic soil grew fruits and vegetables for the mining camps of Hailey and Ketchum.

Then in 1894, Wyoming's Senator Joseph Carey spearheaded a bill through Congress that allotted any western state one million acres to be sold in forty- to 160-acre plots. Priced at fifty cents per acre, the parcels had to be irrigated within ten years. However, under the Carey Act, states could license private companies to build and manage the irrigation projects.

Knowing that if water could make his Blue Lakes property thrive, it could do so for the sagebrush plain, Ira Perrine envisioned a land teeming with lush farms. In 1900, he persuaded Stanley Milner, a Utah banker, to fund an irrigation survey. The study proved Perrine's dream feasible.

Perrine next enlisted a mining broker, who had ties

Blue Lakes, site of Ira Perrine's farm.

to eastern money. Using the financier as his go-between, Perrine sold his scheme to Frank Buhl and Peter Kimberly, Pennsylvania steel barons.

Backed by these wealthy investors, Perrine and Milner formed the Twin Falls Land and Water Company. A Chicago investment bank then raised the money needed to build irrigation canals and a dam across the Snake River.

The State of Idaho granted the Twin Falls Land and Water Company the right to develop 244,000 acres. In 1903, workers broke ground for Milner Dam, launching the South Side Project. Meanwhile, other crews began excavating the Low Line Canal south of the Snake River.

The following year, the company platted the town of Twin Falls. However, when the land office started selling parcels, barely a handful of people stepped forward to buy.

That changed with the completion of Milner Dam. When Frank Buhl shut the gates on March 1, 1905, diverting water into the Low Line Canal, would-be farmers flocked to the land office. City dwellers came too, swelling Twin Falls into a boomtown. Soon, other communities sprang up along the man-made waterway, including two named for the original investors: Buhl and Kimberly.

Almost overnight, the south-river countryside blossomed as though struck by a wizard's wand. It became known as "Magic Valley."

After Frank Buhl and Peter Kimberly declined to back the North Side Project, the Kuhn family of Pittsburgh took their place. From the start, this new undertaking north of the Snake River was beset by problems.

In 1913, a nationwide financial panic threatened to dry up capital. While the Kuhns' fortune dwindled amid plummeting stock prices, Perrine scrambled to keep his work crews paid.

When a planned reservoir north of the Snake River succumbed to the porous soil, Milner Dam proved unable to make up the shortfall. Perrine again saved the day by talking the US Reclamation Service into damming Jackson Lake in Wyoming (now part of Grand Teton National Park). The extra water was a godsend during southern Idaho's torrid summers.

Eventually, the North Side Project brought irrigation to 185,000 acres. By the 1920s, one man's vision had become a showcase for the Carey Act. Through dogged determination, Ira Perrine had transformed the central Snake River Plain into an agricultural mecca that is truly magical.

* * * * *

MILNER DAM: From I-84 Exit 194 (about 20 miles east of Twin Falls and 30 miles west of the I-84/I-86 interchange) drive south 3 miles on Ridgeway Road, turning east on Power Line Road. In 2 miles, merge with Milner Road, keeping right. The dam is 2 miles farther.

CENTENNIAL WATERFRONT PARK: In Twin Falls, drive north on Blue Lakes Boulevard (US 93), turning west at the sign for the Centennial Waterfront Park, 0.1 mile after crossing Pole Line Road. If you're coming from the north, the turn is 0.4 miles south of Perrine Bridge. Follow the main road as it curves right toward the river; one hundred yards later, a street sign will show that you are on Canyon Springs Road. Continue for 1 mile as the road descends into the Snake River Canyon, then swing right at the small sign marking the park entrance; picnic tables, convenience facilities, and a boat ramp lie 0.3 miles beyond. This non-fee park is open from dawn till dusk, year-round.

Numerous trails lead along the Snake River, presenting stunning views of the Perrine Bridge and the basalt-layered canyon. Although Ira Perrine eventually farmed the bottomland on both sides of the river, he located his home near the aquifer-fed lakes on the north shore, the present site of the Blue Lakes Country Club, a private golf course.

PERRINE BRIDGE: Located 0.5 miles north of Twin Falls on US 93. The visitor center parking lot on the south side provides access to the bridge walkways and the north and south rim overlooks. Named for Ira Perrine, the Perrine Bridge was built in 1976, replacing an older span of the same name. It is over one-quarter mile long and arches 486 feet above the water, offering a panorama of the Snake River Gorge that is nothing short of spectacular.

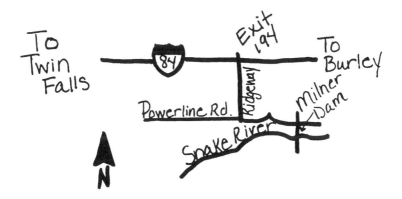

29

Idaho's Lineage of Fire

Saturday, August 20, 1910, dawned hot. In Wallace, Idaho, the sun came up orange, its rays diffused by a brownish-gray veil that overhung the sky like an opaque screen. Out-of-doors, the faint, southwest wind smelled of smoke.

The dry, sweltering summer had witnessed numerous fires throughout the panhandle. That day, a fair-sized one scorched the woods a dozen miles south of town. In the rugged terrain northeast of Elsie Peak, Ed Pulaski, a ranger with the young US Forest Service, supervised crews across several miles of the fire's front.

Near mid-morning the wind gained strength, sending charcoal-colored smoke and gray ash over the Northern Pacific Railroad Depot. Downtown Wallace darkened as though in an eclipse.

At noon the tinderbox forests to the south and west exploded in flame, kindled by the growing wind. The fire raced down hillsides, jumped creeks and gullies, then shot up the opposing slopes. Preheated by the torrid air, acres of timber ignited as though doused with gasoline.

Cut off by the blaze, Ed Pulaski ushered his men into

a mining tunnel. Then, while flames lapped at the entrance, he draped the opening with water-soaked blankets.

Smoke filled the shaft, forcing all but Pulaski on their bellies, their noses and mouths masked with wet rags. Using his hat for a bucket, Pulaski repeatedly flung water at the blankets to keep them from burning. Hour after hour he toiled until exhaustion and smoke finally brought him to his knees, unconscious.

Near dawn a fresh breeze announced that the fire had passed. Awakening from their tomb, Pulaski and his

Old fire damage and new growth in Idaho's panhandle.

men stumbled toward Wallace, leaving five of their number dead from smoke inhalation. All about, the land smoldered, its lush green trees reduced to blackened snags.

At the town limit, Pulaski's crew saw that Wallace too had not escaped. One-third of its buildings—100 structures—lay in ruin.

The Great Fire of 1910 killed eighty-five people. For two days, August 20 and 21, it consumed the Idaho and Montana countryside as though Hell had been set loose on earth. By early September, its smoke darkened Denver,

Memorial to the firefighters who lost their lives in the Great Fire of 1910.

Chicago and Boston. Although President Taft called out the Army to help the fledgling Forest Service, it was the end of the month before rain brought the flames to heel.

Idaho saw 1.7 million acres—an area two and one-half times the size of Rhode Island—go up in smoke. The lumber losses reached billions of board feet.

Today, the Woodlawn Cemetery in St. Maries holds a testament to the Great Fire's human cost. In the back is a circle of stones, marking the graves of fifty-seven fire-fighters who burned to death near the St. Joe River.

* * * * *

WALLACE: Located 47 miles east of Coeur d'Alene alongside I-90; use Exits 61 or 62. Known as the "silver capitol of the world," the town celebrates its early twentieth century mining heritage, and its historical center is a tourist favorite. The old train depot is at Pine and Sixth streets.

ST. MARIES: Located at the junction of State Highways 3 and 5, about 55 miles southeast of Coeur d'Alene. The Woodlawn Cemetery is on West Main Avenue (State Highway 5) at 23rd Street. The firefighters' memorial occupies the back left corner.

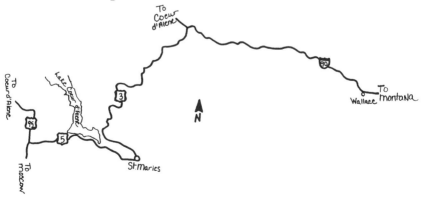

30

AL FAUSSETT'S $733-RIDE
OVER SHOSHONE FALLS

Just after noon on Sunday, July 28, 1929, spectators began gathering on the south bank of the Snake River, a few miles east of Twin Falls. At 5 pm, Al Faussett, a former lumberjack from Monroe, Washington, planned on doing the impossible: riding a boat over Shoshone Falls.

During the previous three years, the lean daredevil had gone over six waterfalls in Washington and Oregon. However, at 212 feet high, Shoshone Falls was to be his most formidable challenge. Faussett's twelve-foot-long canoe resembled an outsized football, its wooden frame covered with orange canvas. Inside, there was barely enough room for Faussett and the half-inflated inner tubes he used for padding.

Legionnaires sold tickets to those wanting to see the stunt up close—fifty cents for adults and twenty-five cents for children. Half the proceeds would go to the American Legion and the other half to Faussett. As the hot afternoon wore on, nearly 1,200 cars filled every flat space between the river and canyon rim. Idaho National Guardsmen, Twin Falls police, deputy sheriffs and Boy Scouts helped with parking and crowd-control. And it

was a good thing they were there, for on three occasions
the Boy Scouts, National Guardsmen and even some of the
spectators had to stomp out grassfires that threatened the
autos.

The crowd eventually reached 5,000, at that time the
largest number of people ever assembled in south-central
Idaho. A few of the more foolhardy climbed atop the boulders sitting gray and dry in the riverbed. In 1929, like
summers today, the Snake's entire flow was diverted into
irrigation canals at Milner Dam.

At 4:30 pm, the Idaho Power Company opened
Milner's gates, releasing a stream for Faussett to ride.
Before climbing into his craft, Faussett rechecked the #12
galvanized wire that ran from a large rock in mid-river,
through a three-inch eyebolt attached to the canoe's bow,

Shoshone Falls in full flow. It looked far different when Al
Faussett went over on July 28, 1929.

and over the falls. Terry Prater sat in a motorboat at the bottom of the falls, holding the wire's free end. A large rocky knob protruded from the face of the falls, blocking Faussett's intended route. When the orange coracle plunged over the falls, Prater was to jerk the wire, guiding Faussett away from the knob.

At 4:45 pm, four detonations signaled that the stunt would begin in fifteen minutes. After stuffing one last inner tube inside the hull, Faussett pulled in his head, and an assistant sealed the canvas shut. Duncan Johnston and Jim Weaver pushed the boat into the river. Even with Milner Dam wide open, the flow was barely deep enough for the craft to float.

Three more explosions marked that there were but ten minutes remaining. A cameraman in a motor launch at the base of the falls steadied himself while he focused his lens on the thin stream of water cascading into space. Nearby, Terry Prater stood up in his boat and pulled the slack from the wire he clutched in his gloved-hands.

Two more blasts warned that there were five minutes left. The crowd pressed forward, each person seeking the best vantage. Johnston and Weaver held Faussett's canoe in a small eddy, ready to shove it into the feeble current.

At exactly 5 pm, a single explosive clap brought down a curtain of silence as the crowd held its collective breath. After wishing Faussett "good luck," Johnston and Weaver pushed him into the current. As the football-shaped boat drifted toward the edge, Prater reeled in slack from the guide-wire.

Above the falls, Faussett's canvas hull scraped over a patch of rock. The boat stuck. Johnston and Weaver waded out to it, then muscled it into a deeper flow. Prater pulled the wire taut, directing Faussett toward the brink.

As the orange bow edged over the falls, the camera-man turned his hand-crank, recording the momentous event for the newsreels. Terry Prater tightened his grip around the wire, waiting to deflect Faussett away from the protruding knob. The crowd dared not blink, lest it miss the plunge.

The canvas boat teetered at the precipitous drop, but refused to go over, having again become stuck. Once more, Johnston and Weaver plodded through the shallows. Buttoned up inside like a canned sardine, Faussett could do nothing but pray.

After reaching the canoe, Johnston and Weaver strained against its stubborn weight, trying to move it without ripping the cloth hull. As the boat inched forward, the rock lip began to act like a fulcrum. Lifting the stern, Johnston and Weaver tilted the bow over the chasm.

And then it was gone. Prater yanked the wire, whipping Faussett away from the worrisome knob. The news photographer cranked the film through his camera, hoping he caught the bow as it shattered against a rock at the base of the falls. The crowd watched, too nervous to talk, knowing that no one could live through such a terrible fall.

Two rescue boats towed Faussett to the south shore, where his orange cocoon was opened. Favoring his right hand, which he had broken, the plucky daredevil stepped out of his boat and waved. A moment later, a salvo of explosions announced that Faussett was safe.

The American Legion sold $1,466 in tickets that day. For his death-defying ride over Shoshone Falls, Al Faussett earned $733.

* * * * *

SHOSHONE FALLS: From Blue Lakes Boulevard (US 93) in Twin Falls, drive east 3 miles on Falls Avenue. Turn north (left) on E3300. In 2 miles, descend to the overlook.

Shoshone Falls is most spectacular in the spring, before the Snake River is diverted for irrigation. However, during the summer and early autumn, it more closely resembles what it was like when Al Faussett took his daring ride.

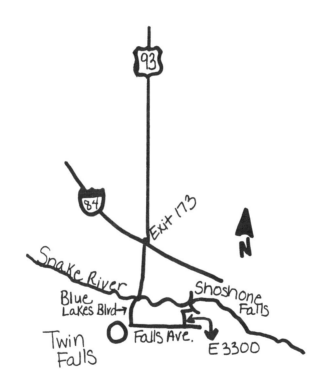

31

SUN VALLEY'S
BANANA BOAT CONNECTION

Mention "Sun Valley," and most people will envision skiers schussing through untracked powder as they link turns down Bald Mountain. A few might also picture a robin's-egg-blue sky and a morning sun transposing the previous night's snowfall into a billion glistening diamonds. But almost no one will think of banana boats.

Yet if it weren't for banana boats, Sun Valley's skiers would be hard-pressed to ascend "Baldy's" 9,150 feet.

In 1935, when Averell Harriman began planning the nation's first destination ski resort, he had no thoughts of banana boats either. As chairman of the Union Pacific Railroad, he was concerned with adding passengers to his company's trains.

Competing railroads, such as the Santa Fe, Southern Pacific and Northern Pacific, could whisk their riders to the Grand Canyon, Coronado or Yellowstone National Park. The Union Pacific had no spectacular sights that could compare.

Having recently visited the Swiss Alps, Harriman had seen skiers flocking to resorts like Zermatt and St. Moritz. But in the United States, skiing was in its infancy.

About this time, Harriman made the acquaintance of Count Felix Schaffgotsch, an Austrian who was working in New York City. In November, 1935, the Count agreed to travel the western United States, seeking a fitting site for a ski resort. Naturally, Harriman insisted that it be located in an area served by the Union Pacific.

Over the next two months, Schaffgotsch eliminated one place after another: Mt. Rainier—too close to Seattle; Mt. Hood—too rainy; Yosemite National Park—too crowded. From Lake Tahoe to the San Bernardino Mountains to Colorado to Utah, the likely locations faded into snowy disappointment.

Then in January, 1936, the Count came to Idaho. Bill Hynes, the Union Pacific representative accompanying Schaffgotsch, showed him the country around Pocatello. The Count admitted there was plenty of snow, but the mountains didn't have the proper scenic backdrop. He and Hynes headed over Teton Pass to Wyoming.

In Jackson Hole, Schaffgotsch saw the peak of his dreams. The Grand Teton reminded him of the summits in his native Austria. Excitedly, he wired Harriman that he had found the spot; the snow and vistas were perfect. However, the State of Wyoming refused to open Teton Pass in the winter, and a southern approach was too far from a Union Pacific railhead. His mission a failure, the Count boarded a train for the East, while Hynes headed to Boise.

The following day, Hynes recounted the fruitless search to his friend, Joe Stemmer, director of Idaho's highways. Stemmer suggested the Count look at Ketchum. The Union Pacific owned a spur line to the old mining town, and Stemmer argued that there had to be enough snow for skiing, since the railroad spent a fortune each winter keeping the tracks clear.

Hynes hurriedly dashed off a telegram, requesting that Schaffgotsch meet him in Shoshone. When the wire caught up with the Count in Denver, he grabbed the next train for Idaho.

Because the winter rail service to Ketchum ran only three days per week, Hynes and Schaffgotsch drove from Shoshone, a gutsy decision since they made the trip in a blizzard. As they rode down Timmerman Hill into the Wood River Valley, their car slid into a snowbank, where it remained until a plow came by and pulled it out.

Upon finally reaching Ketchum, the two men took lodgings in a small, run-down motor court. Unaccustomed to having an urbane guest like Schaffgotsch, the proprietor handed him a shovel so he could dig a path to his cabin.

The next morning, the Count and Hynes awakened to a blue, sun-filled sky. After breakfast, Schaffgotsch put on a pair of skis, which he had brought with him, and climbed atop Dollar Mountain. The view was stunning, and when he skied down, the powdery snow billowed around his head. Two days later, the Count telegraphed Harriman that he had found the ideal setting for the resort.

The Union Pacific chairman arrived in February via his private rail car. Agreeing with the Count that the valley was perfect, Harriman paid $39,000 for the 4,300-acre sheep ranch of Ernest Brass, which was about a mile outside of Ketchum.

In March, Harriman enlisted Charlie Proctor and John E. P. Morgan, two prominent American skiers, to position the resort's ski runs amid the surrounding hills. Meantime, Count Schaffgotsch wandered the ranch with a deck chair as he sought the best views and best sun. After sitting in countless locations, he pointed at a patch of snow-covered ground and announced that the lodge should be built there, in the middle of a hayfield.

While Schaffgotsch, Proctor and Morgan were scouting the ranch, Harriman hired Steve Hannagan, an eastern publicist who had transformed a worthless stretch of Florida sand into Miami Beach. One of Hannagan's first recommendations was to name the new resort "Sun Valley." Unable to imagine why anyone except a crazy person would choose to vacation in the snow, Hannagan insisted that the resort have certain frills that would make the cold "bearable."

As the resort's plans rapidly expanded to include a heated swimming pool, ice rink and bowling alley, the budget ballooned. By the time construction crews poured the concrete for the foundation, the lodge had grown from a $500,000, 120-room hotel to one with 220 rooms, costing $1.5 million. Then as the hotel began to take shape, the architect discovered that the building envelope extended beyond the Brass Ranch. Fortunately for Averell Harriman, the Ketchum Livestock Association, which owned the infringed land, agreed to sell the Union Pacific another 40 acres.

With the hotel construction underway, Steve Hannagan turned his attention to the ski runs, insisting that they be equipped with "mechanical devices" to move the skiers uphill. That someone might actually climb a mountain just to ski down was beyond his comprehension.

European resorts transported their skiers via aerial tramways. In the eastern United States, a few ski areas had the newfangled rope tows and j-bars, whereas Yosemite used an Upski, a six-person toboggan that was winched up while being counterbalanced by an empty, descending toboggan.

Hannagan's suggestion for mechanical ascenders was assigned to the Union Pacific's engineers in Omaha, Nebraska. Two hoists were required, since Charlie Proctor and John Morgan had decided that both Proctor and Dollar mountains should have ski runs.

While several of the engineers began adapting the j-bar and rope tow to Sun Valley's slopes, others examined the feasibility of cog railways. Among the engineers was Jim Curran, who had recently worked for Paxton-Vierling Ironworks, where he designed conveyor hooks that loaded bananas aboard a ship in a continuous flow, rather than one bunch at a time.

As Curran thought about moving Sun Valley's skiers, he couldn't get the banana conveyor out of his mind. If he could substitute chairs for the hooks, he knew he'd be able to carry more skiers than either an Upski or tram. Further, chairs would deliver skiers atop a mountain without the burning thigh muscles that were by-products of the rope tow and j-bar.

After making a blueprint of his idea, Curran showed it to his boss, who felt it was too dangerous. Soon afterwards, Charlie Proctor visited Omaha to check on the engineers' progress. As he flipped through drawings of cog railways and rope tows, he saw Curran's design for the mobile chair and asked the young engineer how it worked.

Intrigued by the concept, Proctor recommended Curran's chair to Averell Harriman, who then asked the engineers to build a prototype. The assignment was given to Jim Curran.

Since no one knew how fast a skier could be safely picked up, Curran fashioned a wooden scaffold on the bed of a Ford utility truck and suspended a chair from its side. Wearing a pair of skis, John Morgan, who had come from Idaho to help, stood on straw while a driver slowly edged the truck and chair toward him. When the skis refused to slide properly, Morgan switched to roller skates.

Beginning at four feet per minute, Curran increased the truck's speed until the chair was snatching Morgan at a brisk seven and one-half feet per second.

On August 26, Curran began constructing his skier conveyors, which he called monocables, on Dollar and Proctor mountains. Since "chairlift" wasn't in the dictionary, the publicist, Steve Hannagan, advertised the devices as "chair-type lifts."

In early November, the first chairlift was ready to test. Twenty female volunteers stepped up to the Proctor Lift, letting its chairs gently pluck them off the ground. Some of the ladies waved to the crowd of onlookers, while others gripped the bars attaching the chairs to the moving cable until their knuckles blanched. Suddenly the lift motor stalled, leaving the women suspended like so many bunches of bananas.

While Curran frantically searched for the cause of the stoppage, workmen lowered the nervous volunteers with ropes. After replacing a blown fuse, Curran called for the ladies to try again. When none came forward, the resort manager ordered his secretary, Florence Law, onto the lift. This time everything worked perfectly, making Ms. Law the world's first official chairlift passenger.

On December 21, 1936, the Sun Valley Resort opened on schedule. Guests included Hollywood producer David O. Selznick and his wife, actresses Joan Bennett and Claudette Colbert, and a host of America's other rich and famous.

The resort lavished its patrons with the finest food and wine, entertained them with a live orchestra, let them swim in a heated, outdoor pool and skate on man-made ice. Sun Valley offered its guests every amenity . . . except snow. It was early January before skiers could use Jim Curran's chairlifts for anything other than a scenic ride.

* * * * *

Sun Valley's banana boat connection:
the Ruud Mountain Chairlift.

THE SUN VALLEY LODGE AND INN are in the Sun Valley Village, one mile NE of Ketchum on Sun Valley Road. Free bus service connects the Village with Ketchum and the ski areas. Reservations: Sun Valley Resort, Sun Valley, ID 83353; central reservations: Sun Valley-Ketchum Chamber of Commerce, P. O. Box 2420, Sun Valley, ID 83353.

BALD MOUNTAIN: Access from either River Run Plaza in south Ketchum or Warm Springs Lodge in west Ketchum. With 78 runs on 2,054 acres, served by 13 lifts (including seven high speed quads), "Baldy's" 3,400 feet of vertical drop offers fun and challenge to alpine skiers and snowboarders alike.

DOLLAR MOUNTAIN: Access from Elkhorn Road in Sun Valley. "Dollar's" four lifts and 13 runs allow beginning skiers to hone their skills before tackling "Baldy."

River Run Lodge at Sun Valley.

SUN VALLEY NORDIC CENTER: Access from Sun Valley Road. This cross-country ski area has 40 km of groomed trails; north of Ketchum, the North Valley Trails System offers another 140 km.

Other activities include snowmobiling, sledding, snowshoeing, ice skating and sleigh rides. Non-skiers can also ride to the top of Bald Mountain, where the views of the snow-clad Pioneer and Boulder peaks are breathtaking. Whatever your sport, don't leave without visiting the 30,000-square-foot River Run Day Lodge, the newest and largest of "Baldy's" three crown jewels.

Although the 1936 chairlifts no longer exist, at the end of Fairway Road in Sun Valley you can see the Ruud Mountain Lift, which was built from Jim Curran's original design.

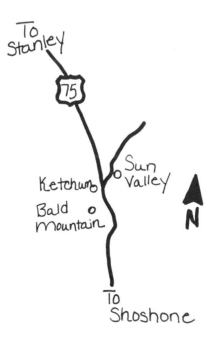

BIBLIOGRAPHY

"Agaidüka, Ancient Fishermen of Southern Idaho." *Cultural Resource Information Series,* Number 2. Bureau of Land Management.

Alt, David D. and Donald W. Hyndman. *Roadside Geology of Idaho.* MT: Mountain Press Publishing Co., 1989.

Ambrose, Stephen E. *Undaunted Courage: Meriwether Lewis, Thomas Jefferson, and the Opening of the American West.* NY: Simon & Schuster, 1996.

Andersen, Shea. "Chairlift Originated in Sun Valley." *Sun Valley Guide,* Winter 1996–97, p. 49.

Andersen, Shea. "Sun Valley: From Harriman to Holding." *Sun Valley Guide,* Winter 1996–97, p. 42–5.

"Another Pioneer Gone Beyond, Heart Trouble Takes 'Rube' Robbins, Trusted Public Servant for Many Years." *Idaho Daily Statesman,* May 2, 1908, p. 5.

"Answers about the Aquifer." Brochure from the Idaho National Engineering Laboratory. Department of Energy.

Arnold, R. Ross. *Indian Wars of Idaho.* ID: The Caxton Printers, Ltd., 1932.

Arrington, Leonard J. *History of Idaho,* Volumes 1 and 2. ID: University of Idaho Press, 1994.

"A Woman Perishes in Snow." *Elmore Bulletin* [Mountain Home, Idaho], May 27, 1896, p. 3.

"Baker Caves." *Cultural Resource Information Series,* Number 1. Bureau of Land Management.

Bluestein, Sheldon. *Exploring Idaho's High Desert,* Second Edition. ID: Challenge Expedition Co., 1991.

Campbell, Mrs. Paul. "Benoni Morgan Hudspeth." *Idaho Yesterdays,* Volume 12, Number 3, Fall 1986, p. 9–13.

Carlson, Dave. "Stark Realities, Craters of the Moon." *Idaho Motorist,* Summer 1995, p. 8–10.

Chittenden, Hiram Martin. *The American Fur Trade of the Far West,* Volumes 1 and 2, 1986 Bison Book Edition. NE: University of Nebraska Press, 1935.

"City of Rocks, Official Map and Guide." National Park Service, 1994.

Coleman, Louis C. and Leo Rieman. *Captain John Mullan; His Life, Building the Mullan Road.* Montreal, Canada: Payette Radio Ltd., 1968.

Conley, Cort. *Idaho for the Curious, a Guide,* First Edition. ID: Backeddy Books, 1982.

Cordes, Jeff. "Sun Valley Lodge Born, The Nine Months of '36." *Idaho Mountain Express,* December 23, 1981, p. C1–7.

"Craters of the Moon Guide." National Park Service, Summer 1995.

"Craters of the Moon, Official Map and Guide." National Park Service, 1995.

"Dare-Devil's Leap at Shoshone Falls Kindles Interest." *Twin Falls Daily News,* July 28, 1929, p. 8.

d'Easum, Dick. "A Bit of a Chill at Atlanta." *Idaho Sunday Statesman,* October 23, 1960, Section One, p. 4.

DeVoto, Bernard. *Across the Wide Missouri.* MA: Houghton Mifflin Co., 1947.

DeVoto, Bernard. *The Course of Empire.* MA: Houghton Mifflin Co., 1952.

DeVoto, Bernard, ed. *The Journals of Lewis and Clark.* MA: Houghton Mifflin Co., 1953.

DeVoto, Bernard. *The Year of Decision, 1846.* MA: Houghton Mifflin Co., 1942.

Dockery, Eva Hunt, ed. "Rube Robbins, Pioneer Marshal, Scout, Indian Fighter—Man Who Never Knew Fear." *Idaho Sunday Statesman,* August 24, 1913, Second Section, p. 3.

Dockery, Eva Hunt, ed. "Rube Robbins and the Silver Creek Duel." *Idaho Sunday Statesman,* August 31, 1913, Second Section, p. 12.

Dockery, Eva Hunt, ed. "Monument to be Erected Soon To the Memory of Rube Robbins." *Idaho Sunday Statesman,* May 10, 1914, Second Section, p. 10.

"East Goes West to Idaho's Sun Valley, Society's Newest Winter Playground." *Life Magazine,* March 8, 1937, p. 20–7.

"Faussett Conquers Shoshone Falls in 'Football' Canoe." *Twin Falls Daily News,* July 30, 1929, p. 8.

Fehrenbacher, Don E. *The Era of Expansion, 1800–1848.* NY: John Wiley & Sons, Inc., 1969.

"Fort Hall, 1834–1856." *Idaho Historical Series,* Number 17, August, 1968.

Frazer, Robert W. *Forts of the West.* OK: University of Oklahoma Press, 1965.

Germain, Jeanette. "Folklore Partly True, Sun Valley Boasts First Chair Lift in World." *Idaho Mountain Express,* December 23, 1981, p. C8–10.

Gray, Shawn. "The Early Years of Sun Valley Resort: Depression, War, Reconstruction, 1936–1950." Private Research Report, May 31, 1985. Courtesy of the Regional History Department of the Community Library, Ketchum, Idaho.

Great Rift, Proposed Wilderness Final Environmental Impact Statement. DC: Bureau of Land Management, 1980.

Grover, David H. *Diamondfield Jack, A Study in Frontier Justice,* 1986 Edition. OK: University of Oklahoma Press, 1968.

Hackett, Dr. Bill, Dr. Jack Pelton, and Dr. Chyuck Brockway. *Geohydrologic Story of the Eastern Snake River Plain and the Idaho National Engineering Laboratory.* DC: Department of Energy, 1986.

Hart, Arthur A. "Famed Indian Fighter Once Kept Boise Peace." Idaho Statesman, June 22, 1970. p. 10.

Hart, Arthur A. "Temperance Movement Enlisted Famous Marshal." *Idaho Statesman,* July 9, 1973, p. 8.

Hart, Arthur A. "They Went That-a-Way." *Idaho Statesman,* December 22, 1975, p. 10B.

Hutchinson, Daniel J. and Larry R. Jones, eds. *Emigrant Trails of Southern Idaho,* Idaho Cultural Resource Series, Number 1. ID: Idaho State Historical Society and Bureau of Land Management, 1993.

"Idaho's Hagerman Valley." Information Sheet, Idaho Travel Council, 1995.

Information Please Almanac, 48th Edition. MA: Houghton Mifflin Co., 1995.

Johnson, Lamont. "The Saga of Peg-Leg Annie." *Seeing Idaho,* November, 1937, p. 18–19.

Josephy, Alvin M., Jr. *The Indian Heritage of America,* 1991 Revised Edition. MA: Houghton Mifflin Co., 1968.

Key, Francis Scott. "The Star-Spangled Banner," America's National Anthem.

Kjelstrom, L.C. "Assessment of Spring Discharge to the Snake River, Milner Dam to King Hill, Idaho." *Water Fact Sheet* of the US Geological Survey, Open-File Report, p. 92–147, 1992.

"Lava Hot Springs." *Southeastern Idaho Tourist Guide,* 1996, p. 58–66.

Lavender, David. *Fort Laramie and the Changing Frontier,* National Park Handbook 118. DC: National Park Service Division of Publications, 1983.

Lecture about Camas by a National Park Ranger at the Spalding Site of the Nez Perce National Historical Park, July 1995.

"Lewis and Clark Trail." Map and Brochure, National Park Service, 1991.

Lindsley, Margaret Hawkes. *Andrew Henry, Mine and Mountain Major.* WY: Jelm Mountain Publications, 1990.

Lopez, Tom. *Exploring Idaho's Mountains.* WA: The Mountaineers, 1990.

Lovell, Edith Haroldsen. *Benjamin Bonneville, Soldier of the American Frontier.* UT: Horizon Publishers & Distributors, Inc., 1992.

Madsen, Brigham D. *Chief Pocatello, The "White Plume."* UT: University of Utah Press, 1986.

"Massacre Rocks Historical Leaflet." Friends of Massacre Rocks.

"Massacre Rocks State Park, Yahandeka Self-Guiding Nature Trail." Guide from Friends of Massacre Rocks.

McPhee, John. *Basin and Range,* 1990 Edition. NY: Noonday Press, 1980.

"Monument at Rube Robbins' Grave To Be Dedicated Decoration Day." *Idaho Sunday Statesman,* May 17, 1914, Second Section, p. 2.

Morgan, Dale L. *Jedediah Smith and the Opening of the West,* 1964 Bison Book Edition. NE: University of Nebraska Press, 1953.

Newman, Peter Charles. *Caesars of the Wilderness, Company of Adventurers,* Volume II. NY: Penguin Books, 1987.

O'Connor, Jim E. *Hydrology, Hydraulics, and Geomorphology of the Bonneville Flood,* Special Paper 274. CO: The Geological Society of America, Inc., 1993.

Official Idaho State Travel Guide. Idaho Division of Tourism Development, 1995.

Ognibene, Peter J. "At the First Ski Spa, Stars Outshone the Sun and Snow." *Smithsonian,* December, 1984, p. 109–19.

Oppenheimer, Doug and Jim Poore. *Sun Valley, A Biography.* ID: Beatty Books, 1976.

Oral Interview with Hilda Goddard of Mackay, Idaho, on January 18, 1996

Oral Interview with Jack Sibbach, Director of Marketing and Public Relations of the Sun Valley Resort, Sun Valley, Idaho, on December 27, 1996.

Oral Interview with Wiley Smith of Mackay, Idaho, on January 18, 1996.

Parfit, Michael. "The Floods That Carved the West." *Smithsonian,* Volume 26, Number 1, April 1995, p. 48–59.

Pawbitse. Interpreted by Herman War Jack. Written by Byrd Trego. "Our Last War with the Paleface." *Idaho Republican* [Blackfoot, Idaho], June 16, 1932, p. 2.

Penson, Betty. "As She Says, Nostalgic Readers Write Footnotes to Local Tales." Letters by Hazel Schooler Rhoades and Maysie Heron. *Idaho Statesman,* July 13, 1975, p. 12C.

Perkins, Barbara, ed. "Sun Valley Lodge Turns 60." *Idaho Mountain Express,* December 18, 1996. p B1 and B3.

Robinson, Russell. *The Story of the Shoshone Indian Ice Caves.* ID: Ice Cave Co., Inc., 1989.

Rozwenc, Edwin C. *The Making of American Society,* Volume I to 1877. MA: Allyn and Bacon, Inc., 1972.

Schwantes, Carlos A. *In Mountain Shadows, A History of Idaho.* NE: University of Nebraska Press, 1991.

Shallat, Todd, ed. *Snake, The Plain and Its People.* ID: Boise State University, 1994.

Smith, Michele McIntyre. "Peg Leg Annie McIntyre." Historical Note, Idaho State Historical Society, April 19, 1991.

"Snake River Canyon." Information Sheet, Idaho Travel Council, 1995.

Space, Ralph S. *The Lolo Trail.* ID: Printcraft Printing, 1970.

Spellenberg, Richard. *The Audubon Society Field Guide to North American Wildflowers,* Western Region. NY: Alfred A. Knopf, 1979.

Stanton, Clark T. "Idaho Indian War of 1878." *North Side News* [Jerome, Idaho], April 27, 1933, p. 1.

"Sun Valley Winter, 1996–97 Season." Information Brochure of the Sun Valley Resort.

Swanson, Earl H. "The Snake River Plain." *Idaho Historical Series,* Number 11, Dec. 1974, p. 1–12.

Taylor, Dorice. *Sun Valley.* ID: Ex Libris, 1980.

"The Snake River Plain Aquifer." Information Pamphlet of the Idaho Water Resources Research Institute, University of Idaho.

Unruh, John D., Jr. *The Plains Across,* 1982 Illini Books Edition. IL: University of Illinois Press, 1979.

Utley, Robert M. and Wilcomb E. Washburn. *Indian Wars,* 1987 Edition. MA: Houghton Mifflin Co., 1977.

"Views from the Visitor Center." Information Sheet, Idaho Travel Council, 1994.

Walker, Eugene H. "A Geologic History of the Snake River Country of Idaho." *Idaho Historical Series,* Number 8, Sept. 1963, p. 1–15.

Welch, Julia Conway. *Gold Town to Ghost Town, The Story of Silver City, Idaho.* ID: University of Idaho Press, 1982.

Whitehead, R.L. "Geohydrologic Framework of the Snake River Plain Regional Aquifer System, Idaho and Eastern Oregon." *US Geological Survey Professional Paper 1408–B,* 1992.

Whitehead, R.L. *Ground Water Atlas of the United States,* Segment 7. VA: US Geological Survey, 1994.

Wyeth, Nathaniel. Wyeth's "stone" quotation taken from a display at the Fort Hall replica in Pocatello, Idaho.

INDEX